"This is a story that needs to be told. It's the story of a life scarred by outrageous injustices. Yet rage was not the end of the story. Father Tolton found happiness and holiness in a life of forgiveness, profound love, and self-giving service. Joyce Duriga has once again shown herself to be a master of popular, relevant, readable biography."

—Mike Aquilina, EWTN host and author of
The Social Doctrine of the Catholic Church

"The timeless tale of Fr. Tolton's life and contributions presented in *Augustus Tolton: The Church Is the True Liberator* will undoubtedly inspire and encourage readers to live authentically as faithful and faith-filled witnesses to the light of Jesus Christ."

—Ashley Morris, ThM
Associate Director
Office of Intercultural and Ethnic Diversity
Archdiocese of Atlanta

People of God

Remarkable Lives, Heroes of Faith

People of God is a series of inspiring biographies for the general reader. Each volume offers a compelling and honest narrative of the life of an important twentieth- or twenty-first-century Catholic. Some living and some now deceased, each of these women and men has known challenges and weaknesses familiar to most of us but responded to them in ways that call us to our own forms of heroism. Each offers a credible and concrete witness of faith, hope, and love to people of our own day.

John XXIII	Massimo Faggioli
Oscar Romero	Kevin Clarke
Thomas Merton	Michael W. Higgins
Francis	Michael Collins
Flannery O'Connor	Angela O'Donnell
Martin Sheen	Rose Pacatte
Jean Vanier	Michael W. Higgins
Dorothy Day	Patrick Jordan
Luis Antonio Tagle	Cindy Wooden
Georges and Pauline Vanier	Mary Francis Coady
Joseph Bernardin	Steven P. Millies
Corita Kent	Rose Pacatte
Daniel Rudd	Gary B. Agee
Helen Prejean	Joyce Duriga
Paul VI	Michael Collins
Thea Bowman	Maurice J. Nutt
Shahbaz Bhatti	John L. Allen Jr.
Rutilio Grande	Rhina Guidos
Elizabeth Johnson	Heidi Schlumpf

More titles to follow . . .

Augustus Tolton

The Church Is the True Liberator

Joyce Duriga

LITURGICAL PRESS
Collegeville, Minnesota

www.litpress.org

Cover design by Red+Company. Cover illustration by Philip Bannister.

3	4	5	6	7	8	9

Library of Congress Control Number: 2018938605

ISBN 978-0-8146-4474-4   978-0-8146-4498-0 (e-book)

America has been called the most enlightened nation. We will see if it deserves the honor. If America has never seen a Negro priest, it will see one now.

—Cardinal Giovanni Simeoni, prefect of the Congregation for the Propagation of the Faith, April 23, 1886

Contents

Foreword

The Catholic Church has been making saints and adding their names to the church's worship calendar for centuries. The church never outgrows the modeling that holy women and men offer to the church militant trying to make a way out of no way in a world of many contradictions. One possibility here is looking back at the African American experience in the United States to discover some individuals tried in the crucible of suffering who might speak as a witness to our times.

Considering the American periods of slavery, legalized segregation, and the corresponding civil rights struggle, no one, black or white, emerges from those human sagas as a saint officially recognized as such by the Catholic Church. There are undoubtedly numbers of such inspiring individuals, black and white, whose stories have yet to be brought to light. Perhaps, our brother, Father Augustus Tolton (1854–97) could be the first or one of the first.

Augustus Tolton says something to us about our handling disappointment, that is, protracted disappointment from minor irritations to outright rejections perpetrated by those we love and by outside forces. The racial climate of the nineteenth century did not offer Tolton much by way of alternatives, a way out of the racial dilemma of that time. He and others took their chances navigating the choppy waters of racial acceptance in and outside the church. It was risky.

He was told the word "no" more often than not and called some names. He could have taken to drink or some maladaptive form of behavior or some obtuse attitude that would have ended with him killed or in jail. But instead, Tolton remained steady in his ministry with a resolve to create a pastoral situation that would offer hope to a people, poor black people.

A Roman collar around the neck of a black man was a news sensation in the black community and an anomaly in the white community. No one had ever seen such a sight in North America. Tolton had a quiet approach and practiced in his priesthood a novel ministry to black and white and was, unfortunately, resented for it. His own bishop replied to a query from Rome by accusing Tolton of creating a situation that was unacceptable in Quincy, Illinois, instead of seeing the evangelical side to this new situation and the advantages it afforded the church by having a priest of African descent. Tolton was a former slave, one who could, to the church's credit, penetrate the hesitations of that era and minister to a people ravaged by the brutality of black slavery but who could benefit from the ministrations, salvation, benefactions, and education the Catholic Church offered.

Tolton had every reason to become embittered. But bitterness was alien to Tolton's soul. Instead, gratitude moved him through to victory. God pulled him through a sinful situation. He was grateful to the church and its priests and nuns who tutored him and advocated to have him recognized by the church for his goodness. His gratitude moved him to declare the Catholic Church the principle instrument for improvement of the plight of the black race following the Civil War and that tumultuous period of putting the country back together in what was known as Reconstruction.

Tolton's holiness stems from his patient suffering, his humble but courageous spirit, and his pastoral heart to all who came to him, both white and black. Tolton's holiness elicits our affection and our empathy; a goodness that attracted people of whatever background to his sermons and ministrations and counsel. His life story inserts a dialectic into a begrudging situation of intransigence to social and moral change, namely, to see dignity inherent in black skin.

I, in turn, am grateful for Joyce Duriga's contribution here to the Tolton record, adding to the small number of qualified reporting on Tolton's life insofar as research has made this available thus far.

We are called to holiness in our own situations. We each have a mission of the cross in life to make a difference, to win this world for God, and to get to heaven. Tolton leaves us a shining example of what Christian action is all about, what patient suffering is all about in the face of life's incongruities. He was a bright light in a dark time. His life and ministry still speak to the problems of our day where communities, neighborhoods, and churches continue to evidence separations among race and class and the disturbances that arise periodically from these social contradictions. Tolton is a model for priests and laity who live and work in these situations.

The uncovering of history has opened up the troubling chapters of a former time in America and in the church. Father Tolton's sanctity comes to light in retrospect through the process of our reflection and our determination to improve our social relations with one another.

Most Reverend Joseph N. Perry
Auxiliary Bishop of Chicago
Vice-Postulator for the Cause of Augustus Tolton

Preface

The life of Father Augustus Tolton could be a Hollywood movie.

Born into slavery on the eve of the Civil War, he escaped to freedom with his mother and siblings when he was just nine years old. Though they were free, the Toltons still lived a humble life working long, hard hours in a cigar factory while taking other jobs to sustain the family. They lived under the threat of the times when blacks were often captured, beaten, and often hanged. At almost every turn, Augustus encountered racism and discrimination but also love and acceptance from some priests and religious men and women in Quincy, Illinois.

Every seminary in the United States turned down his application for priesthood but he didn't despair and was eventually ordained a priest in Rome. But God threw him a curve on the eve of his ordination—he wasn't going to Africa to be a missionary. Rather, he was going back to the United States as the country's first recognized black priest.

He was a sacrificial lamb in some ways, as are all pioneers in history. But he didn't let the racism he faced from fellow Catholics—especially racist priests—change his ardent belief that the Catholic Church was the true liberator for black Americans. He didn't give up or turn away from the church.

Instead he worked harder and gave his all for his flock and it eventually deteriorated his health. He died in Chicago at the age of forty-three.

I first encountered Father Tolton's story through Franciscan Sister Caroline Hemesath's book *From Slave to Priest*. Even though Sister Hemesath used creative license in creating dialogue between Tolton and others that doesn't actually exist, I am grateful for her popular history that introduced me and thousands of others to this powerful story.

My love for Father Tolton was cemented when Cardinal Francis George, OMI, introduced his cause for canonization in the Archdiocese of Chicago in 2011. As editor of the archdiocese's newspaper, I've had a front-row seat to all things Father Tolton ever since. One of the highlights so far was witnessing the exhumation of his body. Seeing his remains made him more real (see appendix 2).

As the story of Father Tolton's life spreads I hope more research comes to light that can fill in some of the gaps in his story, like that of his name. There is evidence of several versions of his first name being used at different times during his life. His baptismal record from St. Peter Church in Brush Creek, Missouri, has no record of a first name. Rather, the entry reads "a slave child," with Stephen Elliot as his owner.

He was likely named after his maternal grandfather, Augustus Chisley. His confirmation record uses the name "August." In Quincy he was called "Augustine" or "Gus." In Rome, "Augustus." For the book's purposes we use "Augustus," which is the name used in his cause for canonization.

A slave's heritage was not considered important enough to write down, so names were incomplete or changed later in life. Slaves were considered property and cataloged as livestock so it is not surprising that records are incomplete. The dates in Tolton's early life have been verified according to documents uncovered prior to the publication of this book. The last name "Tolton" first appears on his confirmation record. At this time, no documentation exists as to where that last name originated. Slaves were not allowed to have last names or use their African names because last names gave a person an identity. Once free, they picked up last names as they moved within society legally or illegally. Some people changed their last names any number of times to avoid recapture, allay discovery, or retain some sense of dignity.

In 1859, five years after Augustus was born, his mother, Martha Jane, and a man named Peter Paul were given permission to marry by their respective owners. It is not believed that Peter was Tolton's biological father but would have been the only father he knew. Father Tolton never mentions Peter Paul as his father in any research discovered to date.

Evidence suggests that Martha Jane is Augustus's mother, but the father could be someone else by the name of Tolton or the name Tolton may have simply been randomly chosen when they were free in Quincy and needed a last name for school and other purposes.

Martha Tolton is worth a story by herself. Her courage in fleeing with her children while being hunted and facing capture never ceases to inspire me and everyone I share the story with. To date there are no recorded conversations with her, but we know she was a woman of faith who stood by her son's side throughout his ministry. "Mother Tolton," they called her. She was a respected figure in the community. I have no doubt that many people sought her advice in the face of life's challenges. I know I would have.

I want to offer a special, heartfelt thanks to Chicago Auxiliary Bishop Joseph Perry, the vice-postulator of Father Tolton's cause for canonization. Throughout the process of writing this book he has been tremendously generous, sharing the research of the cause and answering my many questions.

Heartfelt thanks also go out to Robert Lockwood for his wisdom and advice from beginning to end and to Denise Duriga, Olivia Clarke, Laura Jacksack, Dawn and John Vidmar, and Thomas Howard for their support and help reviewing the manuscript.

It's my hope that through this short book many will fall in love with and be inspired by the story of Father Tolton. He is a man for all Catholics. He was a faithful servant who saw past human imperfections in the Body of Christ to the true teachings of the church that have always proclaimed every life—no matter the race, class, nationality, or creed—is sacred and created in God's image and likeness.

CHAPTER ONE

Flight from Slavery

In the summer of 1863 the United States was in its third year of the Civil War. Just a few months earlier, in January, President Abraham Lincoln issued the Emancipation Proclamation, which declared that all slaves in Confederate states were free people. While the proclamation did not mean owners freed their slaves overnight, it changed the tone of the war to a battle for freedom.

Those changes were felt on the small Elliot plantation in Brush Creek, Missouri. The owner Stephen Elliot died in July, leaving the plantation in debt. In a bid to pay down the debt, Elliot's wife Ann had their property appraised, and that included their slaves. Among the slaves was a family of five—husband and wife Martha and Peter, and children Charles, Anne, and Augustus. Martha was appraised at fifty-nine dollars, Charles at one hundred dollars, Anne at seventy-five dollars, and Augustus at twenty-five dollars.[1] If Ann Elliot decided to sell the slaves it was more than likely that the family would be broken up and sold to different owners. Perhaps it was this knowledge that gave Martha the final courage to flee to neighboring Illinois in a bid for her family's freedom. Knowing that, if captured, she and her children would likely be beaten or killed, Martha—likely under the cover of darkness—rounded up her three children, Charles, Anne, and Augustus, and set out on foot crossing twenty miles of prairie and woods filled with not just vermin, but people hunting runaway slaves.

There is some speculation that other slaves fled with the family but that is unclear. It is also unclear what they had by way of food or protection but they were certainly fleeing for their lives. These were the days when the Fugitive Slave Act of 1850 was still enforced. This law forced non-slaves to participate in the capture of escaped slaves. If they refused, they faced a fine of $1,000 ($32,000 in 2018) and six months in jail. The act also refused slaves a jury trial. Documents from the Elliot estate indicate that the slaves went missing between July and September in 1863. Records from the Elliot estate that year show that Ann Elliot paid ten dollars, about one hundred dollars in modern currency, to bounty hunters to search for the missing slaves. She also took a credit in the final estate settlement for the missing slaves. Later, Augustus recalled the experience in interviews and speeches, sharing that a bounty of $200—about $6,000 in modern currency— was put out for them to be captured dead or alive.

The small family set out for the free state of Illinois and had relatively safe passage until they arrived at the shore of Mississippi River in Hannibal, Missouri, the boyhood home of Mark Twain. On the river's edge, Confederate soldiers accosted the family and tried to arrest them. Luckily, some Union soldiers were nearby and claimed that the spot where the family stood was federal ground and therefore they could cross the river freely. The Union soldiers also helped Martha find a boat to row across the Mississippi River. Once across the river, which at that point would have been almost a mile across, the four refugees were directed to the town of Quincy, Illinois, twenty-one miles away. Quincy was a stop on the Underground Railroad and they would be safe there. Though feeling safe from Confederate troops and those hunting escaped slaves, Martha did not dally on the river's shore. She took her three children and, while probably weary, hungry, and aching with blistered feet, trudged to freedom. Augustus always described his mother as a faith-filled woman, who taught them the Ten Commandments even though she couldn't read. Martha must have been praying to Jesus, Mary, and all the saints for her family's safety. Her courage was remarkable. She did not know what the future had in store, and did not have a husband with her to lean on. What she did have was her faith, her children, and a hope for a better life. That life would include her son Augustus becoming the first native-born American of African descent being ordained for the Catholic Church in the United States.

Martha Jane Chisley, Augustus's mother, was born to Augustus Chisley and Matilda Hurd on the John Manning Plantation in Meade County, Kentucky, just southwest of Louisville. She worked as a domestic cleaning the home and cooking for the family. The Mannings were Catholic and had their slaves baptized and educated in the faith. Martha worshipped with the family—albeit in a segregated section—in a church in Flint Island, Kentucky. In 1849, when the Manning's daughter Ann married Stephen Elliot, Martha was given away as part of the dowry. This meant moving away from her parents to the Elliot's plantation in Brush Creek, Missouri, located about five hundred miles west of Meade County. The Elliots were not wealthy plantation owners and their daughter Savilla gave the slave children classes in the Catholic faith.

Augustus was born April 1, 1854. He was baptized on May 29, 1854, by Father John O'Sullivan, pastor of St. Peter Parish, a log-cabin church in Brush Creek. The entry doesn't have his name, just "a slave child" with Stephen Elliot as his owner. In 1859—five years after Augustus was born—their respective owners gave Martha Jane and a man named Peter Paul permission to marry. Peter Paul was a fellow slave who worked on the neighboring Hagar plantation in the distillery. Given the years between Augustus's birth and the marriage, it is unlikely that Peter was Augustus's biological father but would have been the only father he knew. Later in life, Augustus never referred to Peter as his father.

For his part, Peter Paul decided to enlist in the Union Army. Many male escaped slaves entered into service of the Union and, by the end of the Civil War, it is estimated that around two hundred thousand freed blacks had fought and served in the Union Army and Navy.[2] Most didn't see battle but filled domestic or labor positions. Military records show that Peter Paul enlisted in Hannibal, Missouri, on September 20, 1863, and used the last name Lefevre, that of the priest who baptized him. He entered the Third regiment, Arkansas Infantry, and was five feet six inches tall, aged twenty-five. He died just a few months later on January 12, 1864, at a military hospital in Helena, Arkansas. He never made it to Quincy with his family.

Quincy has a long abolitionist history thanks to bordering Missouri and the fact that Illinois officially abolished slavery in 1824. Home to the Sauk, Fox, and Kickapoo tribes, the first Europeans came to the area in 1818. The city of Quincy was formerly established in 1825, and in 1841 a wave of German immigrants settled there and helped expand the town.

It wasn't unheard of for those hunting slaves to cross the border to Quincy where skirmishes between them and abolitionists ensued. One incident garnered national attention and went all the way to the US Supreme Court. In 1842, Dr. Richard Eells,[3] a physician in Quincy whose home was a stop on the Underground Railroad, was caught helping a runaway slave named Charley flee to the North. Charley swam across the Mississippi River where he encountered Barryman Barnett, a free black man and an agent in the Underground Railroad. Barnett took Charley to Eells who then set out with him in his buggy on the way to a safer hiding place. Along the way they encountered a posse hunting for Charley. Eells told Charley to run and then set off back home to divert their pursuers. The posse soon caught Charley and took him back to Missouri.

Despite slavery being illegal in the state, harboring or helping runaway slaves remained illegal under Illinois and federal law. Eells was arrested and Judge Stephen A. Douglas—who later became famous for debating Abraham Lincoln—heard the case in April 1843, and fined Eells $400 ($12,000 in 2018). The physician appealed his case to the Illinois Supreme Court, which handed it over to the federal courts, saying that only they could rule on cases related to fugitive slaves. In 1853, the US Supreme Court ruled against Eells. The case devastated Eells financially and emotionally and he died before the Supreme Court decision. Illinois Governor Pat Quinn finally pardoned Eells in 2015.[4]

Despite its history of harboring fugitive slaves, most did not make their home in Quincy. When the Toltons arrived, Quincy had a population of about fifteen thousand people, about three hundred of whom were fellow free blacks. This group took Martha and her three children under its wing and found her work cleaning homes and offices. The family moved into Quincy's "Negro Quarter." That same year, Augustus's brother Charles died. He was ten. Augustus, nine, found work in the Harris Tobacco Factory on Delaware near East Street earning fifty cents a week. Then he moved up to a stemmer, a position considered the lowest rung on the ladder where the workers stripped the stems from the large, dried, sticky tobacco leaves. He received six dollars a week as a stemmer for a roller. In the hierarchy of cigar making, rollers rolled the leaves into cigars and earned about five dollars a day. They hired several stemmers to prepare the leaves for them. Tobacco farming and making cigars was labor-intensive work. Nicotine in the tobacco leaves was easily absorbed into the skin of those working with it, causing nausea, dizziness, and nicotine addiction. Tobacco dust filled the air and was especially thick in the summer months, making it hard for workers to breathe. Augustus worked at the factory for nine years.

Eventually the family moved into a small shanty nearer to the Catholic churches of St. Lawrence (later St. Peter) and St. Boniface. In 1868, at the age of fourteen, Augustus took classes at the log-cabin Lincoln School near 10th and Oak streets for three months, when the tobacco company was closed for the winter. His time in the segregated Lincoln School was not a good one for the tall, dark-complexioned youth. Because he could not yet read or write, teachers placed him with the younger children, for which he likely received taunts from the older students. A year later he moved on to St. Boniface School at the behest of the pastor Father Herman Schaefermeyer. That lasted only one month. White parents and parishioners of St. Boniface demanded that Augustus be removed from the school. They wrote letters in protest and threatened to leave the church and withdraw their financial support. The white students also taunted Augustus in class.

Soon after, the Toltons began attending St. Peter Church where they met the pastor Father Peter McGirr. A native of

County Tyrone in Ireland, Father McGirr[5] was a strong man with red hair, fair skin, and freckles. His family was one of the nearly one million who fled Ireland during the Potato Famine of 1845–1849. They made their way to the Quincy area and became farmers. He was ordained for the Alton Diocese, which included Quincy, in 1861. By all accounts, Father McGirr embraced the Catholic Church's view that all people, regardless of class or race, were children of God.

Augustus spent the last four years of his education at St. Peter School, attending during the winter months when he wasn't working at the tobacco factory. He also held a paid position of church custodian. While he was treated well by the priests and the sisters, Augustus endured taunts and slurs by the white students. He graduated from St. Peter's in 1872 at the age of eighteen. Earlier, in 1870, Augustus received his First Communion and confirmation at St. Peter's on June 12, 1870, from Alton's Bishop Joseph Baltes. He was among forty-eight boys and forty-eight girls to be confirmed that day. This is the first public record of the last name Tolton. It was while Augustus was a student at St. Peter's that Father McGirr noticed the signs that the young man may have a vocation to the priesthood. Augustus attended Mass regularly, served in the church, and was generally found to be good, humble, and devoted to the faith.

CHAPTER TWO

Finding His Vocation

For about eleven months in 1875, Martha and Augustus moved to northeastern Missouri where Father McGirr found her a job as housekeeper for his friend Father Patrick Dolan. Father Dolan was to tutor Augustus while he was there. Just traveling to Missouri was a risk because people in former Confederate states were hunting and hanging freed slaves. Some blacks were caught and sold into an illegal slave market in the South.

The Toltons arrived safely but the position didn't last long because Father Dolan was an alcoholic. Mother and son moved back to Quincy and Augustus took a job cleaning a tavern after hours and, during the day, worked at the J. L. Kreitz Saddle and Horse Collar Factory. He still worked as a custodian at St. Peter Church with Father McGirr. Later he found a job making twelve dollars a week at the Deurholt Bottling Company. After seeing what alcohol did to his fellow blacks, Augustus also joined the Temperance Society at St. Peter Church and it is said he never took a drop of alcohol in all his life other than altar wine.

Two years after Augustus graduated from St. Peter School, Father John Janssen from St. Boniface and Franciscan Father Michael Richardt from St. Francis Solano College in Quincy recruited the faith-filled Augustus to help them establish a ministry to Quincy's black community. In 1874, Father Richardt started Sunday catechism classes for the black children and twenty-year-old Augustus was by his side. Augustus knew all of the families so he gathered the children, both Protestant and Catholic. The children enjoyed the classes so much that the idea of a free Catholic school for black children was born. In 1878, they set up the school in unused space at St. Boniface parish. Father Richardt begged the Sisters of Notre Dame from Milwaukee, Wisconsin, to send some sisters to help run the school. They attracted about twenty students to the new St. Joseph School but that quickly grew to over sixty. A Notre Dame sister and a candidate were assigned to the school and taught catechism classes. "The older pupils studied the catechism so diligently that the Holy Sacraments could be administered to them—surely the new school's sweetest and most beneficial fruit. . . . It was a strange sight to see the darkies [*sic*] in white clothes. . . . They were extraordinarily pleased with themselves in white," one of the sisters wrote of the time.[1] Augustus held fond memories of this period in his life. "I was a poor slave boy but the priests of the Church did not disdain me . . . it was through one of them that I stand before you this day . . . it was through the direction of a Sister of Notre Dame, Sister Herlinda, that I learned to interpret the Ten Commandments, and then I also beheld for the first time the glimmering light of truth and the majesty of the Church."[2]

Since many of the students were not Catholic, the success they were having caught the attention of local Protestant pastors. After seven children were baptized the first year the school opened, some Methodist and Baptist pastors held a protest meeting forbidding non-Catholic families from sending their children to St. Joseph School. The Catholic Church was relatively new to the country and Protestant congregations had successfully converted many blacks before and after the Civil War.

The pastors in Quincy made every effort to keep children from the Catholic school. They succeeded and in 1880 the school closed. But the Franciscans and the laypeople wouldn't be deterred. They reopened the space in 1882 as St. Joseph Church and School, the first church for black Catholics in Quincy. It was supported by St. Boniface Parish.

In the early 1870s, several priests of Quincy took on tutoring Augustus to prepare him to enter a seminary. Through them, Augustus studied Latin (the language all seminary classes were taught in), Greek, German, English, ancient and modern history, geography, and philosophy. They also began their quest to get Augustus accepted into seminary. Father Francis Ostrop (pastor of St. Boniface), Father Theodore Wegmann (assistant pastor of St. Boniface), and Father McGirr wrote to every seminary in the country requesting his acceptance and stressing Augustus's ability to read Latin. At the instigation of Franciscan Father Anselm Mueller, who was then president of St. Francis Solano College in Quincy, Augustus enrolled at the college from 1878–1880. There is no indication that he was required to pay tuition. At first the white students from Missouri threatened to leave the school if Augustus stayed. The Franciscans responded that the church did not discriminate against color and they could leave if they wanted. The students stayed and the following year, Augustus was a class leader. Alton's Bishop John Baltes supported Augustus's pursuing a vocation to the priesthood. The *Chicago Journal of History* reported Bishop Baltes saying, "Find a seminary which will accept a Negro candidate. The diocese will assume the expense."³ In America in the 1870s, eighteen seminaries existed—most operated by religious communities but none by Franciscans. All responded that they weren't ready to accept a black, or in their words "Negro," candidate.

Father Wegmann reportedly wrote to the Mill Hill Fathers, later known as the Josephites, who were English missionaries serving Africans in the British empire. It was thought that they were setting up a school to train missionaries for blacks in the United States. In his letter to the Mill Hill Fathers, Father Wegmann had this to say of Augustus:

> I make bold to apply to you in behalf of a young man of the African race, who is very desirous of becoming a missionary for the people of his race, and to whom I have been giving instructions for about a year and a half, having been requested to do so by his Pastor, Reverend Peter McGirr of St. Peter's Church of this city. The young man in question is about 20 years of age, of an excellent character, and of good talents. Studying Latin for over a year, he reads Nepos and Caesar without difficulty—and some weeks ago I have begun Greek with him. I am very willing to direct his studies yet for some time, if I see a prospect for him of attaining the end he aims at, i.e., the sacred priesthood—if I know of a college that is prepared to admit him afterwards.⁴

The Mill Hill Fathers also said they would not accept young Augustus for seminary training. Just a few years later, the Mill Hill Fathers experienced a separation within community ranks, not because of the decision to ordain black Americans but because of a tension over its missionary activities: Was it to recently freed slaves in America or foreign missions in the far-flung British Empire that was the original intent of founder Cardinal Herbert Vaughan?

The newly separated American congregation of the Josephites established St. Joseph Seminary in Baltimore in

1888 to train men who wanted to serve the community's apostolates to blacks in America. They trained Charles Uncles, the second American-born, identified black priest ordained in the United States. Father Wegmann's request on behalf of Augustus Tolton came ten years too early.

Around this time, Bishop Baltes wrote to the Urban College in Rome on Augustus's behalf. Urban College was part of the Congregation for the Propagation of the Faith, also known as Propaganda Fide, whose purpose was to evangelize people around the world. At that time, America was considered mission territory and therefore under the auspices of the Propaganda Fide. Urban College trained men from around the world to be missionary priests. In his letter, Bishop Baltes called Augustus "more than ordinary." "It is impossible to be admitted as a student in any seminary of America, the same reasons do not exist in Rome. If he will be able to be received by the Propaganda Fide, I will contribute voluntarily, in case of need, to the expense of his education," the bishop wrote.[5] In 1876 the Propaganda replied, accepting Augustus as a seminarian but the happy news was never communicated to the priests or to Augustus. It is uncertain whether the letter never arrived or, if it did, that Bishop Baltes changed his mind about sending Augustus to seminary. It was reported that Bishop Baltes tried again during his annual *ad limina* visit to Rome but had no success. (Every few years, bishops from certain geographical areas around the world are required to visit the Vatican to report on efforts in their dioceses. These are called *ad limina* visits.) On his return, the bishop wrote a letter to Father Richardt, not Augustus himself, saying he was unsuccessful and urged them to wait until the Mill Hill Fathers opened a seminary in America. In the meantime, Augustus continued working and helping out with the catechism classes and at the church in his free time. Augustus attended daily Mass, sometimes serving at two Masses in two churches each day, worked at the bottling company, taught catechism, and attended classes at the college.

In no way giving up, Father Richardt from St. Francis Solano College asked the Franciscans' US minister provincial Father Vincent Halbfas to appeal for help to the community's minister general Very Reverend Bernardin of Portu Romano in Rome. Father Richardt described Augustus as a reverent acolyte serving at Mass, a son devoted to his mother, a faithful worker, a diligent student, and a zealous lay apostle. The young man's love of the Eucharist was apparent and he was known to frequently stop into churches as he passed and spend time before the Blessed Sacrament. Father Halbfas wrote to the minister general on October 28, 1879:

> Allow me to propose to the kindness of Your Paternity a petition concerning a young man of black skin color. He desires, because he is destitute of all means of support, to continue his studies in some College in Rome, Naples, or elsewhere . . . in order afterwards to be able to work as a missionary for the salvation of his people. From the enclosed documents it is clear that he is worthy of protection and assistance. Therefore I ask Your Paternity for the love of God that you do not deny the aforesaid young man your intercession toward the completion of the desire of his heart.[6]

The minister general took up the cause and succeeded in getting Augustus admitted to the Urban College. Ten years had passed since the first appeal to seminaries. Augustus was now twenty-six.

No doubt it was a joyous time filled with hope and jubilation. Their prayers to the Lord were answered. His mother Martha and sister Anne, who may or may not have been married by then, probably gathered around him, fussing and helping him prepare for the journey. His friends, both priests and laypeople, also probably turned out to share the excitement and wish him well. Tickets had to be purchased for the train to the East Coast then the ship passage to Europe. Augustus must have experienced some trepidation as well. Never before had he traveled so far or alone. Also, he believed that after six years of study he would move to Africa and spend his life there as a missionary. He might never see his family and friends again. But he put his trust in the Lord. He was going to be a priest.

Those around him rallied to get him ready, even donating money for his expenses. Bishop Baltes gave him fifty dollars and the students and Franciscan friars at St. Francis Solano College took up a collection that netted ten dollars. Throughout Augustus's time in Rome, Father Francis Ostrop, a former pastor of St. Boniface, would send him regular letters and spending money. Carrying a letter of presentation for the college, Augustus boarded a train in Quincy on Sunday, February 15, 1880, bound for Chicago. After a short layover in the Second City, he caught a train east to New Jersey and the port of Hoboken where he arrived two days later. Augustus had friends in Hoboken who invited him to stay until his ship sailed. The Sisters of the Poor of St. Francis operated St. Mary Hospital in Quincy and had a hospital in Hoboken. Sister Perpetua, whom Augustus knew from Quincy, now worked at the hospital and sent the invitation.

On Sunday, February 21, a week after he left Quincy, Augustus boarded the ship *Der Westlicher* bound for Le Havre, France. Twelve days later, on March 4, he arrived in France and took a train to the southern coast to board a ship to Italy. He finally arrived in Rome on March 10. He reported to the seminary on March 12, 1880. Augustus was on his way to realizing the dream God put in his heart.

CHAPTER THREE

The Catholic Church and Slavery

Tolton's time in Rome would have given him a break from the racism he faced every day in Quincy. Since its beginnings, the Catholic Church taught that all people were God's children no matter what their class or skin color. However, this teaching was not always embraced by its bishops, as evidenced in America before and after the Civil War.

As far back as the 1500s, popes publicly denounced slavery, calling it a sin. In 1839, when the issue of slavery was prominent in American society, Pope Gregory XVI released a letter condemning slavery:

> We warn and adjure earnestly in the Lord faithful Christians of every condition that no one in the future dare to vex anyone, despoil him of his possessions, reduce to servitude, or lend aid and favor to those who give themselves up to these practices, or exercise that inhuman traffic by which the Blacks, as if they were not men but rather animals, having been brought into servitude, in no matter what way, are, without any distinction, in contempt of the

rights of justice and humanity, bought, sold, and devoted
sometimes to the hardest labor.[1]

If there was any doubt about his meaning, the pontiff made
his thoughts clear in the letter's last sentence, which reads,
"We prohibit and strictly forbid any Ecclesiastic or lay person from presuming to defend as permissible this traffic in
Blacks under no matter what pretext or excuse, or from
publishing or teaching in any manner whatsoever, in public
or privately."

Just two years after Father Tolton's ordination, in 1888,
Pope Leo XIII vigorously denounced slavery in his encycli-
cal *In Plurimis*, and applauded Brazil's abolishing slavery.
No doubt Augustus would have been drawn to these documents during his time as a seminarian and probably studied
them even if they were not part of his course work. During
his time in Rome, Father Tolton formulated his lifelong
conviction that the Catholic Church is the true liberator of
black Americans.

The Catholic Church in the United States was not a
staunch voice against slavery. In *Passing for White: Race,
Religion, and the Healy Family, 1820–1920*, biographer
James M. O'Toole writes:

> Bishop John England of Charleston actively defended the
> maintenance of slavery where it already existed. Writing
> in his diocesan newspaper in 1840 and 1841, England
> presented a series of open letters addressed to a political
> figure who had, the bishop said, wrongly associated the
> Catholic religion with abolitionism. The charge was a cal-
> umny, England asserted, reviewing the history of slavery
> as presented in the Bible and the writings of the church
> fathers to show that Catholics found nothing inherently
> wrong with it. John Hughes, the archbishop of New York,

considered slavery merely a "comparative" rather than an absolute evil. It was, he never doubted, "infinitely better than the condition in which [Africans] would have been, had they not been seized" and brought to America in chains.[2]

During the time of the Civil War and after, the United States was considered mission territory so dioceses were under the auspices of the Vatican Congregation for the Propagation of the Faith, the same congregation that operated the college that accepted Tolton to the priesthood. Members of the congregation were very aware of the issue of slavery in the United States and the treatment of black people freed following the Civil War. Since 1829, bishops in America held periodic gatherings or councils to discuss issues facing the burgeoning church. However, until after the Civil War, slavery and the treatment of blacks was never addressed because American bishops were divided over the issue. Some bishops, religious communities, and institutions supported slavery and even owned slaves, despite the unwavering church teaching against it.

Archbishop John Spalding of Baltimore was key to getting the bishops in America to face the issue, even though they, in the end, did not take any action. Archbishop Spalding was born in Kentucky to a family who owned slaves. While he believed slavery was a great social evil he wrote to the Propaganda Fide that liberating the slaves would ruin society because experience showed that the "liberated ordinarily become miserable vagabonds, drunkards, and thieves. . . . Such emancipated ones are lost in body and soul."[3] However, Archbishop Spalding seemed truly concerned over the welfare of freed blacks. Perhaps he was fulfilling a promise he made upon graduation from the American College of Louvain,

France, when the rector asked him to dedicate the first years of his ministry to the long-neglected black people.

Either way, Archbishop Spalding reached out to the Propaganda Fide in Rome asking for a council to address how the church could care for emancipated slaves. The Propaganda Fide agreed and appointed Archbishop Spalding as its delegate. Archbishop Spalding proposed discussion on the care of freed blacks but also of the appointment of a bishop to oversee their spiritual care. "In the former, the proposals considered special churches for African Americans, African American priests, and missionary endeavors among blacks. The latter dealt with the creation of new dioceses and candidates for the episcopacy, and with the advisability of creating a prefect apostolic to oversee the spiritual work on behalf of African Americans on a national level."[4] Rome approved the agenda, which included a discussion about how to evangelize black Americans. The reception from US bishops was less than enthusiastic, especially on the point of evangelizing freed blacks.

The Second Plenary Council of Baltimore began October 7, 1866—three years after the Toltons escaped slavery—but due to the inability to accomplish all it set out to do, discussion on appointing someone to oversee the spiritual care of blacks was held over to an extraordinary session that started October 22. The bishops discussed the topic at length with not a little bitterness. In 1865, at the end of the Civil War, it is estimated that there were 100,000 black Catholics in the United States. That number grew to 138,000 by 1889.[5]

Archbishop Spalding did not reveal that it was his idea to appoint someone to oversee the spiritual care of blacks in America and that it should be a bishop. The last part upset Archbishop Spalding's brother bishops. The archbishop of New Orleans said he would continue to care for the black people in his archdiocese but no more measures were needed. The bishop of Savannah disagreed. He urged the appointment of an "ecclesiastical man." The bishop of St. Louis said he would resign from his office if he was told to accept a bishop for blacks.[6] Other bishops said that while they may have many blacks in their dioceses, few were Catholics. At the end of the Second Plenary Council nothing had changed. No bishop was appointed to minister to emancipated slaves and no new programs or plans were adopted to reach out to this vulnerable population on behalf of the Catholic Church in the United States. Instead, they endorsed the practice of bringing missionaries from Europe to work among the black population.

While the US bishops made no headway, the Vatican, having a long memory, did not drop its interest in the plight of freed blacks in America. Eighteen years after the council in Baltimore—during the same time Tolton was a seminarian at Urban College—officials from the Propaganda Fide called for a Third Plenary Council of Baltimore to specifically address the issue.[7] In 1883, Cardinal Giovanni Simeoni, who would later decide that Tolton would return to Quincy, called the archbishops from the Unites States to Rome for a meeting in November. He was prefect of the Propaganda Fide. The congregation had twelve concerns it wanted the bishops to address during a new council—a priority was ministry to the freed people. They noted that little had been done for emancipated slaves since the last council. Rome also proposed a special collection in parishes that would benefit missions to blacks in America.

The Third Plenary Council of Baltimore opened on November 9, 1884. "After much discussion the council decided that one collection would be taken up in all dioceses on the first Sunday of Lent for Indians and Negroes, the money to be sent to a special commission composed of the archbishop of Baltimore and two bishops who were to be appointed."[8] One of those bishops would be James Healy of Portland, Maine, born of a slave mother and a white father but who did not acknowledge his African heritage. The collection is still conducted today. The bishops also called for seminarians to be encouraged to work among black people and, again, that religious men and women be encouraged to undertake the work.

CHAPTER FOUR

The Healys

The year Father Tolton was born, 1854, was the same year the first black, native-born American was ordained a priest. His name was James Healy but he did not identify with his heritage and, being light-skinned, assimilated into the white community. This was also the case for two of his brothers—Sherwood and Patrick—who also became priests. The Healys are worth noting because they were contemporaries of Father Tolton and would have heard of him once he was ordained. It is unclear but likely that Father Tolton knew of them. Black Catholics at the time knew of the Healys, even if the brother-priests eschewed any involvement with them.

All three brothers rose to prominence during their lifetimes. James became bishop of Portland, Maine, and Patrick became the twenty-ninth president of Georgetown University in Washington, DC, and is called the school's "second founder." Sherwood was a seminary professor and trusted aide of Boston's Bishop John Williams. None of the brothers recognized their African heritage and managed to be accepted into white society. James and Sherwood, in particular, had noticeable African features but still managed to hide their background with the help of friends around them.

The Healy brothers were three of ten children born to Michael and Eliza Healy in Macon, Georgia. Michael owned a prosperous plantation and had a monogamous, long-term relationship with his light-skinned slave Eliza. They considered themselves married although that was illegal at that time. Even though her children had both races in them, back then any "drop" of African ancestry made a person black and therefore in that place and time, a slave. Knowing that this threatened and limited his children's existence, Michael shipped them north to boarding school as soon as he was able. There they would have opportunities but they wouldn't have their parents. After leaving Georgia there is no evidence that the boys thought of their mother or tried to contact her. Over time, ties to Georgia weakened, but the ties between the siblings as they moved around the North grew strong. There is little evidence that Michael or his children ever thought they would return to Georgia. If they ever returned they would be considered runaway slaves.

Around 1837, Michael sent James, and later his sons Hugh and Sherwood, to New York City where he enrolled them in a Quaker school. The Quakers were staunchly against slavery and believed all God's children were equal no matter their race. Michael traveled often for his businesses and knew people in New York. He asked his friend and colleague John Manning to look out for his children. Manning became like another parent to them. In 1844, on a business trip north where he also planned to check on his sons, Michael met someone who would safeguard and secure the futures of his children—John Fitzpatrick, a Catholic priest and newly appointed auxiliary bishop of Boston (two years later he would become bishop of Boston). The Healys were not Catholic, but Fitzpatrick encouraged Michael to send the boys James, Hugh, Sherwood, and Patrick to the newly opened College of the Holy Cross located in Worcester, Massachusetts, that was staffed by the Jesuits. The four boys entered in the fall of 1844. This new journey was a turning point in their lives, and for three of them, launched them on the path to priesthood. At the end of the college's year-opening retreat, all four boys were baptized along with two other students. Just seven months later they received the sacrament of confirmation from Bishop Fitzpatrick.

Based on the brothers' personal writings, their conversions to Catholicism made a powerful impact. "James spoke for all of them. In 1849, he looked back on the occasion and recognized it as the decisive event of his life. 'Today five years ago,' he wrote, 'I entered this college. What a change. Then I was nothing, now I am a Catholic,'" writes Healy historian James M. O'Toole. "The others too were profoundly affected. Patrick would speak of his conversion as the opening of 'a new and more perfect life,' while Sherwood was described as 'wonderfully altered.' All four brothers immediately enlisted as altar boys, and when James assisted at Mass, the experience touched him deeply: 'how the thought of it awed the soul,' he wrote in wonder."[1]

One historian explained their conversion as going from the frying pan into the fire. They were already living a difficult life as children of a mixed-race union during the time of slavery and now they joined a church that in America was viewed with suspicion and nativist attacks. It was at this time that the brothers consistently began separating themselves from blacks and any association with them. They found an established community and connections when they entered the church. All were particularly bright and excelled in academics. The brothers spent holidays with families of priests they met. While James, Sherwood, and Patrick went into seminary—Patrick with the Jesuits—Hugh went into trade. Bishop Fitzpatrick arranged for their sister Martha to live with his own sister.

On June 10, 1854, just two months after the birth of Augustus Tolton, James Healy was ordained a priest for the Diocese of Boston. His mixed race was always lurking in the background and Bishop Fitzpatrick considered it when finding a place for Father James. The priest himself wondered if America was the place for him or if he should minister abroad. In the end, Bishop Fitzpatrick put Father James out in plain sight and appointed him as the first-ever chancellor of the Diocese of Boston and his personal secretary. Because dioceses in the United States were growing, bishops were mandated to create "chanceries" or offices to deal with things like construction projects, personnel issues, and finances. This made Father James second in command and very prominent. If anyone had complaints about Father James's heritage, they did not dare to make them public.

Around this time, Sherwood was getting ready to enter a seminary in Rome. Because of his questionable background on such things as whether or not his parents were legally married, Bishop Fitzpatrick stepped in and glossed over some of the details for entry. He would do that again. Sherwood was ordained in December 1858, but again Bishop Fitzpatrick did not know where to place the Healy brother especially since it looked like America was headed toward civil war. He sent Father Sherwood back to Rome for more studies. After receiving a doctorate in canon law (the official law of the church), Father Sherwood came to mind for a position as rector at the new American College being established in Rome to train priests from the United States, now known as the North American College. In a letter to Archbishop John Hughes of New York, Bishop Fitzpatrick shared his dilemma. He felt Father Sherwood eminently qualified for the position but felt his ancestry would be a problem. "He has African blood and it shews [*sic*] distinctly in his exterior. This, in a large number of American youths, might lessen the respect they ought to have for the first superior in a house," the bishop wrote.[2]

Back in Boston, Father Sherwood stood out among his fellow priests not just because of his features but because he was very well educated. For a time he administered a home for orphans then served as chancellor while his brother, James, went on a European vacation. This all occurred during the Civil War but based on his journals and notes it doesn't seem that Father Sherwood took particular interest in the conflict. In 1862, he joined the faculty of St. Joseph Seminary in Troy, New York, to teach moral theology. In 1865, Bishop Fitzpatrick died and was succeeded by Bishop John Williams. The new bishop took Father Sherwood on as a personal aide and adviser, taking him to the First Vatican Council in Rome and to the Second Plenary Council of Baltimore where the bishops of America discussed life in the church following the Civil War and how to minister to freed blacks. On the latter, Father Sherwood remained silent.[3]

Father Sherwood's health was never strong and while in Rome for the council, he became very ill and it was thought he would die. However, he recovered and when returning to Boston took on what was thought to be lesser duties as rector of the cathedral. However, a new cathedral was under construction and Father Sherwood oversaw those details along with the fund-raising for the project. Eventually he was made pastor of the largest parish in Boston, but it all took its toll on his health. On October 21, 1875, he died at the age of thirty-nine.

What is remarkable about Father Sherwood, maybe more than his other priest-brothers, is that his parishioners and even the local news media that covered his funeral knew of his ancestry but did not comment on it publicly. "The reality that had governed his entire life and career—the 'African blood' that 'shewed'—remained unacknowledged. In the process, that reality itself was obscured. Readers who did not know him would conclude simply that an Irish Catholic priest (of which there were many) had died. . . . By acting as if the disabilities imposed on African Americans did not apply to him, he forced others to respond in kind, and his life thus upsets our historical generalizations about race in the United States," historian O'Toole notes.[4]

A few months before Father Sherwood died, his brother James was appointed bishop of the Diocese of Portland, Maine, which at the time included all of Maine and New Hampshire. When his dossier was sent to Rome for approval, once again details surrounding his ancestry were glossed over or omitted. Notably during his tenure as bishop, from 1875 to 1900, Bishop Healy attended the Third Plenary Council of Baltimore (1884) where American bishops, at the request of Rome, gathered to address how to minister to freed blacks and Native Americans. Having many tribes established in his diocese, Bishop Healy championed the cause of Native Americans, even encouraging his state to open schools for them, but on the topic of freed slaves he remained silent. During this time, Tolton was a fourth-year seminarian in Rome at the Urban College.

Just a few years later in 1889, black Catholics gathered for a similar meeting for the first time as the Colored Catholic Congress (the predecessor of today's National Black Catholic Congress). Organizer Daniel Rudd, publisher of the national black Catholic newspaper, the *American*

Catholic Tribune, sought endorsements and attendance from bishops they felt would be sympathetic to the cause. One of those was Bishop Healy. "That they wrote to him at all is telling, an indication that his racial background was widely known, even if it was never discussed openly. . . . His response to the idea of a 'colored congress' was predictably cool. He was 'much obliged' for the invitation to attend, he told the organizers, and 'I wish you all success for the convention.' "[5] Bishop Healy used his health as the reason for not attending. He used the same reason the two other times the organizers invited him to congresses.

In 1892, Father Tolton visited New England and spoke in Boston. While race was never mentioned in newspaper articles related to the Healys, it was at the forefront of those covering Father Tolton. "To say, as the *Pilot* did, (the newspaper for the Diocese of Boston) that Tolton was 'the first American Negro' ordained to the Catholic priesthood was to say that James Healy, who had been ordained thirty years before him, was not a 'negro.' . . . To say that Tolton was a black man was to say that James Healy was not," O'Toole writes.[6]

Like his two brothers, Jesuit Father Patrick Healy was well-respected for his intelligence and academic achievements. Because he had more European features than his two priest-brothers, Father Patrick chose to distance himself geographically from them and went to teach at Jesuit-run Georgetown University in Washington, DC, in 1866. In 1873 he was named president of what was then the largest Catholic college in the United States. Racism was strong among the Jesuits in America at the time. Some Jesuit houses would not permit Father Patrick to stay with them when he traveled because of his ancestry, and Georgetown itself owned slaves.

Just like his brothers, Father Patrick did not identify with his African ancestry and so ignored it. He is credited with expanding Georgetown from a small liberal arts school to a major university. He revamped the law and medical schools and changed the student body. In the past, most of the students came from wealthy Southern families. With the collapse of many family fortunes following the Civil War, Father Patrick recognized the school needed to look farther afield for students. He turned to the North where an influx of Catholic immigrants was flooding into the cities. Father Patrick also oversaw the start of new construction and the majestic Healy Hall, which is today a national landmark and the flagship building on campus. Often called Georgetown's "second founder," Father Patrick resigned from his presidency in 1882 due to failing health. He died on January 10, 1910. Today the university publicly acknowledges Father Patrick as an African American.[7]

The Healy brothers' success at passing for whites is just one more complicated chapter in the history of race and the Catholic Church in America.

CHAPTER FIVE

Tolton Goes to Rome

Within nine days of arriving at Urban College in 1880, Tolton and his other first-year classmates were inducted and received the college's black cassock with red sash and black biretta with a red tassel. One hundred forty-two young men from around the world were studying to become priests alongside Tolton.

Pope Urban VIII established the college that would bear his name—Urban College or Urbaniana—in 1626 to train men from around the world to be missionary priests. It was a pontifical university tied to the Congregation for the Propagation of the Faith, also called the Propaganda Fide, established by Pope Gregory XV in 1622.[1] The university still exists today and is under the Congregation for the Evangelization of Peoples, formerly the Propagation of the Faith. They now also train men and women religious and lay-people to work as missionaries. During Tolton's time the priests were ordained as secular, meaning they worked alongside diocesan priests and reported to the diocesan bishop, not to a religious community like the Benedictines or Franciscans.

Racial prejudice did not noticeably exist at the college or in Rome. Tolton found the Italian professors "lovely and fatherly," especially professors Checci, Conrado, and Levi. "All were my friends," he said, "they loved me though I cannot say why."[2] During his time he also mastered the accordion and would play spirituals for his classmates. Some people from Quincy corresponded with Tolton during his time in seminary. His mother was illiterate but it is likely his sister Anne kept in touch as much as they could, given the price of paper and postage, and it is known that a few of his priest friends did too.

In the archives of the Congregation for the Evangelization of Peoples (formerly known as Propaganda Fide) exists a class roster listing Tolton as a student at the college. Augustus Tolton is listed as student number twenty-five. Next to his name is written the Diocese of Alton, that he was of the Latin Rite, his birth date of April 1, 1854, the date of his entry into the college, March 12, 1880, that he was enrolled in third theology, that he took the Propaganda Oath May 6, 1883, and that he was a deacon. This roster establishes without a doubt that Tolton was a seminarian at the college. It also reveals information about his fellow seminarians.[3] They hailed from various rites—Syrian, Chaldean, and Maronite, for example—and from various countries such as Syria, Cyprus (which at that time was under British rule), Greece, Australia, Sri Lanka, countries in Africa, and the Middle East, to name a few. Another American appears on the roster—James MacGloin from Buffalo, New York.

In the book, *The American College in Rome: 1855–1955,*[4] Robert F. McNamara describes the life for the average seminary student in the Eternal City in 1867, just twelve years before Tolton started his studies at the Urban College. Life in Roman seminaries was very similar and the American

College, now called the North American College, at that time closely followed the rule set by the Urban College. Dormitories typically had beds made of planks connected to iron head and footboards and mattresses filled with dried cornhusks. Seminarians were provided sheets, blankets, and washbowls along with desks and kneelers.

Tolton spent his days within his camerata, or a group of about twelve men divided by where they lived in the dormitory. This tradition dated back to the seventeenth century and each camerata was led by a prefect and vice-prefect who were upperclassmen appointed by the seminary and selected for their leadership abilities or other talents. Cameratas did not mingle within the seminary, except on special occasions. "They took their daily walks together, in double file," McNamara writes. "Not only was the destination selected by these officers but—at least in those days—the partner with whom each camerata-member would walk."[5] In the evenings they would gather in a "camerata-room" for entertainment and relaxation.

Along with the other seminarians, Tolton received his allotted uniform of cassock and sash, soprana (wide-brimmed, three-cornered hat), biretta (traditional box-shaped hat with a tassel on top), zimarra (cloak), and shoes made from a cobbler. The men were also given a shirt, pants, stockings, and handkerchiefs. Chewing tobacco snuff was common among Italian clergy, McNamara says, so they were given extra handkerchiefs for that, even though many Americans—like Tolton—didn't take to the habit. Laundry was sent out.

On days he had classes, Tolton would rise before 6 a.m. in time for a meditation in the chapel followed by a low Mass. Those were the days of Tridentine Mass, which was used until 1964. Mass was said in Latin with the priest facing the altar, away from the congregation. During high Masses, the priest and congregation chanted or sang the Mass parts. In the low Mass these were read. Only on Sundays did he receive Communion, as was the prevailing custom of the time. He also went to confession weekly.

Students typically ate a traditional, light Italian breakfast of coffee and rolls then headed off to classes, which began at 8 a.m. Before lunch they had two classes, a study hour, and made a brief examination of conscience in the chapel. All classes were in Latin. Lunch was the largest meal of the day. Afterward they had two more classes and a study hour. Then back in the chapel for the rosary and spiritual reading. Dinner was at 8 p.m., then time for recreation and night prayer at 9:30 p.m.

The building where classes were held dated back to the seventeenth century. One of its features was a painting of St. Philip Neri talking to a young man. It was titled *E poi?* (which translates to "And then?") and was a reflection on eternity. (St. Philip Neri lived in the 1500s and founded the Congregation of the Oratory, or Oratorian Fathers.[6] He is called the "third saint of Rome," after Sts. Peter and Paul.) Classes were often held in a large lecture hall with "hard, initial-carved desks and harder benches."[7] Most of the instructors were clergy from the Diocese of Rome, but some belonged to religious communities.

During public meals, Tolton and his fellow classmates listened to spiritual reading. A student would climb to a pulpit in the refectory or cafeteria and read aloud from an assigned book or text. Sometimes on special occasions the rector would cut the reading short and allow Tolton and his classmates to talk to each other. Once the sun went down, students were in for the night. "Roman ecclesiastical custom decreed that the Ave or Angelus, which rang at sunset, should be considered as a curfew for clerics," McNamara explains.[8] While students did not have classes on Thursdays, Sundays, or holidays, those days were often filled with mandatory walks and religious services.

At Urban College, Tolton learned the ins and outs of liturgical ceremonies and was taught to sing or play an instrument. Tolton, whose fellow students called "Gus," enjoyed the rich devotional traditions in Rome during Advent, Christmas, Lent, and Easter. The feast of the Epiphany on January 6 is the highlight of the Roman Christmas season, and Urban College marked it the following Sunday with a day of speeches from the seminarians in over forty languages.

It is not clear what Tolton did during the summer months in Rome. Some seminaries had country houses that students could visit and get out of the city. During his six years in Rome, Tolton would have surely attended Mass with Pope Leo XIII in St. Peter Basilica and heard him deliver annual messages in the square at Christmas like the *Urbi et Orbi* blessing on the city and the world. The St. Peter's of Father Tolton's day is very much like the St. Peter's of today with the large square out front, Bernini's columns flanking the basilica, and the obelisk in the center of the square. Inside, Father Tolton would have stood over St. Peter's tomb taking in the masterpiece of Bernini's baldachino with the angels, large and small, suspended as if holding the piece over the large altar. Perhaps he spent time in prayer before Michelangelo's *Pieta* or staring up at the ceiling of the Sistine Chapel.

Rome breathes Christian history in the ruins, palaces and churches, and the catacombs where early Christians worshipped and were buried. The many relics of saints who lived there can be venerated. Tolton saw all of these and took in the universality of the church. He also would have drunk in the richness of the city's history and culture: the festivals, piazzas where people gathered, outdoor markets, galleries, and gardens, to name a few. Black faces were not uncommon in Rome so people wouldn't stare at him as he passed by and would not bar his entry anywhere. It was an experience that transformed him but also left him a little lonely.

Six years of intense study finally brought him to his goal of ordination to the Catholic priesthood. But on the day before ordination, he received word that he would not go to Africa. Rather, his new mission territory would be Quincy and the United States. Cardinal Giovanni Simeoni, prefect of the Congregation for the Propagation of the Faith, made the announcement: "America has been called the most enlightened nation. We will see if it deserves the honor. If America has never seen a Negro priest, it will see one now." Cardinal Simeoni was the cardinal who, just a few years earlier, ordered the bishops in America to address the issue of ministering to freed black people. Even after deciding to send Tolton back to the United States, college officials doubted he would be successful, given the country's racial prejudices. Someone had to be the first black priest and Cardinal Simeoni decided it would be Tolton.

The next day, Holy Saturday, April 24, 1886, at the Basilica of St. John Lateran in Rome, Tolton was ordained by Cardinal Lucido Maria Parocchi, prefect of Urban College. As is the tradition still today, people lined up inside and outside the basilica to receive a "first blessing" from the newly ordained priests. Father Tolton must have been jubilant. He finally reached his heart's and spirit's desire to be a priest for God. At the same time he knew how difficult his new ministry would be and what he would be up against as the first native-born, recognized black priest in the United States. But he picked up that cross in obedience.

The following day, Easter Sunday, Cardinal Simeoni arranged for Father Tolton to celebrate his first private Mass over the tomb of St. Peter in St. Peter's Basilica. The temporary altar set up for the occasion stood in front of the personal altar of the pope. How thrilled and humbled Father Tolton must have been. The first time a priest celebrates the Eucharist is not something he ever forgets. For his first Mass, Father Tolton celebrated over the tombs of St. Peter and other popes, the site of countless pilgrimages and in the mother church of the Catholic faith.

He recalled his first time offering up "the White Host" five years later in the *American Catholic Tribune* on April 11, 1891:

> The glorious Easter-tide is now coming before us once more, if I live to see it, if it's God's will to suffer me to stand before the sacred tabernacle Easter morn, it will be my fifth year offering up the White Host to the living God. How swiftly will not my thoughts go back to the great Cathedral of St. Peter's in Rome, where on Easter Sunday, 1886, I arose with the glorious thought in my breast that I am now a priest; that I must now betake myself to the tombs of Saints Peter and Paul, where there was an altar in readiness for me to offer up for the first time, the White Host to God over the bodies of those two great saints, buried under the dome of the glorious St. Peter's?
>
> Then when I was saying "Gloria In Excelsis," my thoughts would jump to the shores of America, when I would say "Oremus." My thoughts would go to my dear old home, where I expected to go after three months would elapse, then it was that I beheld Quincy in my imagination. God has permitted me, in his allwise providence, to sing many "Glorias" in my old home for four years; many "Glorias" in Chicago for one year, in which time no doubt I have offered up many a prayer for the welfare, for the

conversion, and for the blessings of Almighty God upon
my people.

Easter Sunday I will imagine to be standing again in St.
Peter's at Rome over the tombs of those Apostles, who gave
their lives and their time to save the people. God grant that
I may persevere faithful to the end in this holy state of life,
so that when called to render an account of my steward-
ship, I may as a priest forever appear willingly before the
Eternal Priest, our Lord himself.

His expression shows a heart and vocation focused outward on the people to whom he felt called to minister. Much
like the two apostles he mentions, Father Tolton himself
would give his life and his time to "save his people." From
Cardinal Simeoni from the Propaganda Fide in a note in its
files dated June 3, 1886: "Father Augustine [*sic*] Tolton is
now about to leave for Alton, Illinois, his diocese in America.
Although he is not profoundly learned, he is nevertheless
trustworthy and willing, alert and obedient. Please allow
220 lira to pay for the journey to America. The amount he
has, 485 lira, is not sufficient."[9] Father Tolton left Rome on
June 13, 1886. It was the feast of Pentecost, the "birthday"
of the church when the Holy Spirit descended upon the
apostles following Jesus' resurrection and launched them
out into the world to spread the Good News of the gospel.
On the day of Father Tolton's departure, the rector of Urban
College's seminary wrote this in his notes: "Without much
effort he is naturally endowed with great talent. A black
man from America, self-effacing, pious and with other virtues sufficient to be commended. He is sufficiently prepared
and quite capable for the missions, but seems to be preoc-
cupied by contradictions by chance experienced in part by
his domination in America."[10]

Three days following Father Tolton's departure, officials
from the Propaganda Fide sent a letter to the Diocese of Alton

and its vicar-general, Father John Janssen, who was also pastor of St. Boniface Church at that time, informing them that Father Tolton was returning to serve there. Church leaders in Rome expressed doubt that Father Tolton would succeed in his ministry given what he was up against in America.

Unbeknownst to Father Tolton, Bishop Baltes died in February 1886. Father Janssen, who knew the new priest well, was serving as administrator. "Reverend Augustus Tolton, an alumnus of the College of the Propagation of the Faith and a priest of this diocese, since he will already have completed his course of studies, ought to return to this diocese. Further, we consider it opportune to offer you information regarding his talent and capability. He has shown himself praiseworthy both in his activity in acting and in his spirit of obedience toward his superiors in such a way that his superiors were able to confide in him," Propaganda Fide officials wrote. "Although he might not greatly excel in knowledge, nevertheless he is strong in the understanding of his intellect and acquiring experience under the prudent and keen direction of matters which have to be done, in the space of time he can fruitfully labor in the vineyard of the Lord. As for the rest, he is pious and industrious."[11]

Father Tolton traveled from Rome to the nearby coastal suburb of Civitavecchia. From there he took a boat north 162 miles to Livorno, Italy. During his stopover there, an Italian immigration officer mistook Father Tolton, who spoke fluent Italian, for an Italian citizen from Africa and tried to enlist him in the army. Father Tolton recalled the experience in a letter he sent to the Propaganda Fide from Quincy in September 1886:

> I left Rome on the day of Pentecost with two other persons and went to Civitavecchia. The next day when the ship arrived we went aboard to go to Livorno. At this place an

Italian immigration officer wanted me to enlist, that is, take service on the warship. I refused but he came to me a second time and began to prod me again and again until I told him I was an American. Instantly he left me alone. He, this officer, thought I was an Italian subject (Massua) [*sic*] because I spoke Italian. In Marseille we were put under quarantine for 24 hours. From then on everything went well for the remainder of the journey.[12]

From Livorno he set sail for Marseille, France. He likely traveled by train north to catch a boat across the English Channel to Liverpool, England. During a twelve-day layover in Liverpool, an Irishman on the ship befriended Father Tolton and took him back across the channel for a brief tour of several countries. The man arranged for Father Tolton to celebrate Mass in several basilicas. Back in Liverpool, Father Tolton set sail to America on the *Gallia*, arriving in New York on July 6, 1886.

His first Mass on American soil took place on July 7 at St. Mary's Hospital in Hoboken with the Sisters of the Poor of St. Francis. He was fulfilling a promise to Sister Perpetua made before he set sail for Rome. That Sunday he celebrated Mass at St. Benedict the Moor Parish in New York City. This historic congregation, located on Bleecker Street in Greenwich Village, was the first Catholic Church for blacks north of the Mason-Dixon Line. Before heading for Illinois he again visited the Franciscan sisters in Hoboken, New Jersey, and offered Mass for them.

CHAPTER SIX

Back to Quincy

Upon receiving word that Father Tolton was heading home, Father Peter McGirr—the young priest's mentor and pastor of St. Peter Church—organized a homecoming. He chartered a train car to take Father Tolton's friends east to Springfield to meet the new priest upon his arrival. They traveled together back to Quincy. As the train arrived in Quincy, a brass band played "Holy God We Praise Thy Name" and a crowd of thousands greeted him and cheered. He boarded a decorated carriage with four white horses that drove him through town to St. Peter Church where another large crowd greeted him.

On July 17, 1886, Father Tolton celebrated his first Mass in Quincy at St. Boniface Church, where he often served Mass and where, at one time, he was removed from classes after racist taunts from children and racist threats from parents. "The grandest service ever held in Quincy, we believe, was held in St. Boniface yesterday morning, the occasion being the first Mass in Quincy by Father Tolton, the first colored American priest of the Catholic Church." So read the report of the *Quincy Daily Journal* for July 19,

1886. The community of the southern Illinois town was in alt over the historic event. It was a day of jubilation.

Both blacks and whites packed the church for the Mass. White and red streamers suspended from the center ceiling flowed out to the columns along the sides of the church's interior. Red and white streamers also floated down from the reredos on the back of the altar out into the sanctuary area of the church and into the congregation. Perhaps the red was a nod to the red sash and red tassel on the biretta of priests ordained from Urban College. The church's side altars were decorated with red and white flowers, and small candles lit up the altar for Mary. Delicate ivy twined around the columns of the altar "and a profusion of chaste flowers rested upon the superaltar," the *Quincy Daily Journal* reported. A delicate white cloth was draped over the tabernacle and ivy, roses, and white veiling decorated the altar cross.

Father Tolton sang the high Mass in Latin. A Franciscan friar from the nearby college served as master of ceremonies. Ten priests and two friars sat in the chancel, the area near the altar reserved for priests or choirs. Father Anselm Mueller, rector of Quincy's St. Francis Solano College where Father Tolton once studied, preached the sermon about the role of the priest to sacrifice himself for his people. He is to be a teacher, a mediator, and a healer, Father Anselm said. "Rejoice today because another priest has been given to us," Father Anselm preached. The beauty and majesty of the occasion moved the reporter from the *Quincy Daily Journal*. "To even the Protestant visitor the altar aglow with lights, the richly robed priests and the gorgeous ceremony was impressive. . . . Father Tolton has the full, rich and musical voice common to his people, and his intoning at the altar can be heard distinctly throughout the church." Father Tolton recalled the day in a letter to the Propaganda Fide a few months later. "In America all received me well, especially the Negroes, but also the whites—German and Irish. I celebrated Mass on July 18, and in the Church of St. Boniface, with 1,000 whites and 500 colored people present. Everybody cheered: 'Long live the Propaganda.' I was graciously received by the Episcopal administrator, Bishop Janssen, who appointed me pastor of the Negro Church of St. Joseph (Quincy)."[1]

St. Joseph Church was part of St. Boniface Parish, which let the congregation use the buildings rent-free. A former Protestant church, the small church building was seventy by thirty-six feet and was all theirs. Oil paintings of the Stations of the Cross lined the walls, and shrines to the Blessed Mother Mary and St. Joseph flanked the altar. St. Boniface offered to sell the building and the school to St. Joseph's congregation for $3,000 ($74,000 in 2018), but that was still unaffordable to the poor, black community.

Father Tolton wasted no time getting started. On Sundays, he said two Masses and led Vespers and catechetical instruction. He also offered Mass daily and held religious instructions in the school. On Saturdays from 2 to 9 p.m. he heard confessions. Weekday afternoons and evenings he taught the faith to those wanting to be baptized. He counseled those who sought his guidance, and made home visits, especially to the sick and aged. The remaining time he worked on his homilies and recruited students for the parish school. From the start, people were drawn to the young priest. The secret of his pastoral success seemed to be in his innate simplicity and genuine love that he openly expressed to everyone he came in contact with. He spoke often of his time in Rome.

Integration came naturally to Father Tolton, who saw blacks and whites coexist peacefully in Rome. Regular parish groups formed such as a girls' choir with both black and white members, and an altar society of eighty women also of both races. His Masses were standing room only—with both blacks and whites attending together—and black and white boys often served together on the altar. His catechism classes for non-Catholics were also reportedly well attended. St. Joseph Church was full each Sunday and Father Tolton was "highly esteemed by all and everyone likes his sermons," one priest wrote to a family member.[2] Father Tolton and his mother, who served as parish sacristan, lived in an apartment on Eighth and Maine streets. It is unclear but likely that Anne Tolton lived with them.

An average of sixty children attended St. Joseph School and many children were baptized. However, at least in the winter months, many of the children attended school just to have a warm place to go. Blacks in Quincy were very poor. The parish often provided shoes, clothing, and food to the children. While many were baptized, not all carried on in the faith.

People of both races stood in line to go to confession and get spiritual advice from Father Tolton. He was active in the community, especially in the struggle against alcohol abuse, which was rampant among poor blacks. But Father Tolton knew firsthand that his people had many issues in their lives such as unstable work, poor work conditions and pay, alcoholism, and much more that made their attendance at Mass inconsistent. Many were also probably coping with their new lives as free people after slavery.

The American Catholic press took note of the country's first recognized black priest. The *American Catholic Tribune* ran a large photo of Father Tolton on its front page on

March 11, 1887, with the headline "Rev. Augustus Tolton: The most conspicuous Man in America." "He has made friends among all races there [in Quincy], and as he passes through the streets white gentlemen raise their hats to him as readily and reverently as they do to other priests, for they have imbibed from the Catholic Church the knowledge that we are all sons of God and brothers of Christ the Lord," they wrote.

The *St. Joseph's Advocate*, an annual publication produced by the Josephites, expressed doubt that Father Tolton would be successful in Quincy, "since no man is a prophet in his own country. The servant is not above his master and let us not expect from this poor sacerdotal servant a miracle which his Master did not work. Nay, we are prepared in this relation for any degree of failure in Quincy, though morally certain, seeing the Finger of God in his whole past, of ample success elsewhere." The notoriety made the young priest uncomfortable. The *Advocate* sold copies of the priest's portrait, which upset him. "I never wanted them, neither for myself nor anybody else, not even for my mother," Father Tolton told the publication.[3]

While no letters or interviews with Martha Tolton have been discovered, it is clear that she was active in her son's ministry throughout his life. The community called her "Mother Tolton," a term of respect. There is one report in the *American Catholic Tribune* of her intervening when a girl at their parish and school was being harassed by her anti-Catholic, Methodist aunt and guardian. The aunt would ridicule the Catholic faith in front of her niece, Martha Nevada Brown, and would bring the Methodist pastor over to lecture her. When he arrived Martha would lock herself in her room, which enraged the aunt who would threaten to break the door. "She [the aunt] finally decided to take her from the Catholic school and send her to the public school, to this Mrs. Tolton, her god-mother [*sic*] objected. Mrs. Tolton claimed that as god-mother, she had a right to look after the spiritual welfare of the child, and had the child to come and live with her. The aunt claimed that she had the best right, at all events the girl would not live with the aunt, and vowed and declared that nothing would ever move her from her faith," the *American Catholic Tribune* reported.[4] Martha Tolton won the day and welcomed Martha Nevada Brown into their home. Later the girl expressed a desire to become a religious sister and Father Tolton helped her enter the Oblate Sisters of Providence in St. Louis, Missouri.

CHAPTER SEVEN

Trouble Begins

Despite the town's initial acceptance of Father Tolton, not all were happy with his ministry, especially clergy from other faiths who opposed or feared the spread of "Romanism" among the people. These groups actively worked against Father Tolton, whether in public or in secret. Father Tolton lamented his lack of success among the black community. Within just one year of his arrival, the priest was questioning whether he would better serve his people in another city. Bishops from Chicago, Cincinnati, and Galveston, Texas, had written to him requesting he come and serve their black Catholics.

From the beginning of his ministry, Father Tolton was committed first to his congregation. While being offered paid speaking engagements around the country he often turned them down because he didn't want to neglect his parishioners by being away too often. Travel itself would not have been easy. Train cars were segregated and if there wasn't enough room in the black cars, those patrons had to stand. It could also be dangerous since tensions between blacks and whites increased following the Civil War and

Reconstruction with the advent of Jim Crow laws that introduced and enforced racial segregation.

Since priests ordained for the Propaganda Fide had to regularly send reports to Rome updating officials on their ministry, in July 1887, Father Tolton expressed his frustration to the Propaganda Fide. "During the year that I have been pastor the number of Negro Catholics has not increased; it seems they do not care much for religion. The majority of the Negroes here are Baptists and Calvinists and many are Masons. I had only six conversions. The Negroes in Chicago complain that they do not have a Negro priest and that I am here in Quincy. They have asked their Archbishop—[Patrick] Feehan, to procure from Rome my transfer to Chicago," he wrote.[1]

He requested their permission to leave. But there was more going on in Quincy. "There is also a priest here who accuses me of wasting my time. Your Eminence, please decide for me whether I may go or not. The Germans and the Irish helped me a lot by supporting my Church and they too want me to stay here. Other people from neighboring parishes go around selling my picture to make money. This is being done without my consent and with my displeasure. They also want me to go elsewhere and preach for money," he wrote.[2]

The Propaganda Fide replied, telling Father Tolton to stay in Quincy and continue his work. Responding to a letter from Baltimore's Cardinal James Gibbons, Father Tolton shared some of his frustrations over the lack of support from Catholics in America for more black priests. Throughout his ministry, Father Tolton encouraged his fellow black men to become priests.

> I must say, most dear Cardinal, that I have never found a companion of my color since I have returned from Rome, consequently I don't think there is a second colored priest

yet. I have been trying to find out, but I cannot find it anywhere. I would be here proud if a second one could be found in America; but thanks be to God I have been able to send one in my place in Rome. Mr. William Reed from St. Vincent Abbey West Moreland, Pennsylvania. He is doing well but it pains me that I am not able to send him much only 20 dollars in 2 years time.

How Father Tolton found the money is not known because he shared in the letter that he was not receiving a salary from the church or the diocese.

I hear of so many places of well disposed [*sic*] colored people being without any priest sometimes I really wish I could go to all of them, but I am alone have been working hard in Quincy to get these colored people but all in vain so far two years hard work but the grace of God is wanting then they are ill disposed. I have only 31 souls in all mostly women, of course must work many ways to keep them from going astray; but now it happens that I am drawing all the white people here from 1 to 200 whites attending regularly that is fine for me, but it causes a little jealous feelings among other neighboring brother priests, of course they say the white people have white priests enough without going to the negro or as they said, "nigger" priest.

He praises Quincy's white people, saying they, for the most part, were good-hearted, charitable, and not prejudiced.

It had to be a difficult time for Father Tolton. Priests were seen in society as separate from their flock, and, at the time, above them. He couldn't really have true friendships with his brother priests who were white because of the class divisions in society, regardless of good intentions. His mother was always by his side serving in his church and keeping up their home, but she too could only relate to a certain extent.

Adversities in his parish and community continued to mount. At first, many whites came forward to help the impoverished parish. While some came just to see the black priest, others were sincere in their faith. It was common to see white penitents in line for confession at St. Joseph's. Gradually, many stopped attending likely because of pressure from others with racial prejudice.

To make matters worse, the parish's friend and advocate Father Theodore Bruener, pastor of St. Boniface, was transferred to another parish. Faced with a large debt, the new pastor, Father Michael Weis, resented the generous donations his white parishioners made to St. Joseph's Church. As dean of the Quincy area, Father Weis insisted that Father Tolton, whom he referred to as "that Nigger priest," minister only to blacks. But Father Weis didn't stop there. He publicly declared that any money white Catholics put into the collection basket of St. Joseph belonged to St. Boniface.

The situation reached a tipping point in late 1888, early 1889, when Father Tolton performed the wedding for one of Quincy's wealthiest daughters against her family's wishes. Her mother objected to her marriage to a man she found unacceptable and managed to ensure that none of the white parishes married the couple. Despite Father Tolton's following proper church procedures and even receiving approval from the young woman's pastor, Quincy's elite society was incensed by the wedding and turned against the black priest. When Father Tolton asked St. Boniface's Father Weis for advice, he was rebuked and told to leave Quincy. Father Weis had the ear of the new bishop, James Ryan, who, after the incident, told Father Tolton to minister only to blacks or leave the diocese. Father Weis's persecution continued to rattle Father Tolton, who was in a tough place and could not publicly respond to the racist priest because of the inequality between the races.

After this, Father Tolton sent another letter to the Propaganda Fide begging to leave the Alton Diocese. It was dated July 12, 1889—nearly two years to the date he celebrated his first Mass in Quincy: "There is a certain German priest here who is jealous and contemptuous. He offends me often and hurts me deeply. He abuses me in many ways and asks that I leave and has told the bishop to send me away. I would gladly go elsewhere just to be rid of him. The bishop too has given me this advice."[3]

Mention of the bishop stirred the Propaganda Fide to send a letter to Bishop Ryan, asking if what Father Tolton wrote was true and did he want him out of his diocese. Bishop Ryan sent the following response:

> The Reverend Lord A. Tolton has indeed worked with very great zeal in this diocese; he is a priest remarkable both for his piety and diligence. However, because I have observed that his special mission has been marked out by the Propagation of the Faith, it is in no way possible to form a congregation of blacks in Quincy. He himself admits this and it agrees with the opinions of his fellow priests in Quincy. There results an impossibility of forming a congregation of blacks in Quincy because of the scarcity and difficulty of stable conversion. Otherwise, the Reverend Lord Tolton has happily conducted the matter, he has a good reputation among Catholics and non-Catholics and everywhere he is he creates an impression favorable to religion.

What is not written in the letter and what likely upset the bishop, the white priests, other clergy, and the town's elite was that a parish that invited blacks and whites to worship together was naturally forming. It was natural to Father Tolton since it was what he saw firsthand in Rome. It was also something the people of Quincy weren't ready for.

Despite Bishop Ryan's response, officials at the Propaganda Fide told Father Tolton to "keep up the good work" and "you must understand that given the great difficulties your project may not be fulfilled immediately."[4] They felt the bishop's praise of Father Tolton was enough.

But Father Tolton did not give up and wrote more letters to the Propaganda Fide during these months, begging permission to move to Chicago, where black Catholics specifically requested that the archbishop write to him. The tone of the letters shows Father Tolton's increasing distress. Father Weis, referred to in these letters as the "blessed German priest," must have been increasing his persecution of Father Tolton.

> I am again writing to your Eminence to ask permission to join the Archdiocese of Chicago with Mons. [*sic*] Feehan. . . . I can only say: "Deo Gratias" I am really begging your eminence to give me permission to go also because I do not want to stay with this blessed German priest and also Bishop Ryan thinks that it is best for me to go with Monsignor Feehan . . . I am writing to your eminence out of need. In this nice city of Quincy since about a year ago we experienced a deep change that almost caused the destruction of the entire congregation because here we have a very peculiar German priest. No other priests like him because he is always arguing and writes to the bishop for anything. I never met such a jealous and inadequate priest. He told the bishop that: "It would be better if Tolton leaves" because his parishioners—the ones of the German priest—go to the black church, as he calls it.[5]

The large number of white people who worshipped at St. Joseph's is what angered Father Weis, he said. About thirty-five blacks and two hundred whites regularly attended services. "This German priest is very bitter: he is full of hatred against me. To keep the peace, the bishop has asked me to look for another diocese," Father Tolton wrote. "I will always say that the white people in Quincy are true Christians and not just the shadow they are very generous and very lovely. Lately four white soldiers came to me for confession. They had not been receiving communion for 25 years but they had a wonderful confession and touched by God's grace they kept coming to my church."[6]

He no longer had the heart to stay. Bishop Ryan gave him permission to move to Chicago. Not hearing soon enough from the Propaganda Fide he wrote yet another letter begging to leave.

> At that point I will be out of the persecution from this priest . . . and then he says that he cannot do anything with his people because they all go to the black church. I cannot deny that many come to my church but they come from all over the town and not just from his church and this is what all the other parishes are saying. But he says that if it was not for this my people would go to their [white] church. There are five other churches in this town and for this reason he has no reason to say this. I think this is a case of jealousy and nothing else and for this reason the farther I can be, the better . . . not just for me.

Finally, Father Tolton's prayers were answered with a letter from the Propaganda Fide dated November 7, 1889, granting its consent, which it turns out was not needed in the first place. The oath that priests of the Urban College took allowed them to serve anywhere within the province— or geographic area containing several dioceses. The Archdiocese of Chicago and the Diocese of Alton were within the same province. The *Quincy Daily Journal* reported his transfer on March 12, 1888:

> Rev. Aug. Tolton, the colored priest of this city, and priest in charge of St. Joseph congregation, Seventh and Jersey streets, notified his congregation yesterday morning that he had received notice from Rev. Father Jansen, administrator of the Alton diocese, to the effect that he would be sent out to do missionary work for the next two weeks, and at the expiration of that time would probably be transferred to some other city. The announced was entirely unexpected, and caused deep sorrow to the church members, who will probably have to attend services at the other Catholic church after this. It is to be hoped that the authorities will decide to let him remain in this city.

Upon departing from Quincy, at least in public, Father Tolton maintained his history of humility and kindness and did not reveal the real motivation for his departure to Chicago.

The *Quincy Daily Journal*, November 13, 1889, quoted a letter Father Tolton wrote to a personal friend about his move, expressing thanks to his white benefactors who sent him away with some donations to help him set up his life in Chicago. They requested his prayers and promised to work three times harder and donate three times more money to his ministry if he would remain with them in Quincy. "Catholics will love and respect a priest regardless of nationality; at least that is the spirit of those people in the Gem City who knew me for twenty-nine years or more. Never will they forget the happy hours spent in the little St. Joseph church," he wrote. "I wish them all the blessings that can be bestowed upon them, for that charitable spirit that they have always shown toward me and the colored children."

CHAPTER EIGHT

His Friend, Daniel Rudd

By the nature of his being a priest and black, Father Tolton did not have many close friends or contemporaries but one of those men was Daniel Rudd, founder of the national black newspaper, the *American Catholic Tribune*, and founder of what is today the National Black Catholic Congress.

Rudd was born on August 7, 1845, in Bardstown, Kentucky, to slave parents Robert and Elizabeth Rudd. His parents were Catholic and he and all of their eleven children were baptized. It is unclear how Rudd's faith became so important to him but it is clear that it did. "I have always been a Catholic and, feeling that I knew the teachings of the Catholic church, I thought there could be no greater factor in solving the race problem than that matchless institution whose history for 1900 years is but a continual triumph over all assailants," Rudd wrote in his newspaper.[1]

Following the Civil War, he moved to Springfield, Ohio, where his brother lived and where he attended high school. In 1885, he began his first newspaper, the *Ohio Tribune*. Later that year he expanded its mission and changed the name to the *American Catholic Tribune*, the first national

Catholic newspaper owned and operated by a black man. "We will do what no other paper published by colored men has dared to do—give the great Catholic Church a hearing and show that it is worthy of at least a fair consideration at the hands of our race, being as it is the only place on this Continent where rich and poor, white and black, must drop prejudice at the threshold and go hand in hand to the altar."[2]

Several American bishops endorsed his newspaper and he listed them on the masthead: "Cardinal Gibbons, archbishop of Baltimore, Md., the most Reverend Archbishops of Cincinnati and Philadelphia, and the Right Reverend Bishops of Covington, Ky., Columbus, O. [*sic*], Richmond, Va., Vincennes, Ind., and Wilmington, Del."

Each issue averaged four pages targeting literate black Americans. He also had whites among his subscribers. Correspondents in various locations like Fort Wayne, Indiana, New England, and St. Louis, reported on news at various times around the country. For one period a black seminarian from the Urban College wrote from Rome. In 1886, Rudd moved the publication to Cincinnati. In addition to stories from correspondents, the newspaper reprinted stories from other newspapers, which was customary for small newspapers at the time. Some of these stories featured coverage of lectures Father Tolton gave in various towns. Subscriptions and advertisements did not cover the cost of the newspaper's publication so Rudd raised funds through donations. Revenue from a printing company in their Cincinnati office also defrayed costs.

Rudd was both a journalist and an activist. He featured news relevant to black Americans and championed the rights of blacks, writing editorials opposed to segregation and discrimination in all of its forms. As violence against blacks increased in the 1890s and hangings became more prevalent,

Rudd spoke out against Americans' inaction over these atrocities.

Throughout his editorials and features, Rudd's mission and philosophy came through: "The Catholic Church alone can break the color line. Our people should help her to do it."[3] On another occasion he wrote: "The Negro of this country ostracized [*sic*], abused, downtrodden and condemned, needs all the forces which may be brought to bear in his behalf to elevate him to that plane of equality which would give him the status he needs as 'a man among men.' . . . We need assistance and should obtain help whenever and wherever it can be given. The Holy Roman Catholic Church offers to the oppressed Negro a material as well as spiritual refuge, superior to all the inducements of other organizations combined."[4]

However, he was not blind to the discrimination black Catholics experienced at the hands of white Catholics and expressed that within his newspaper. Rudd saw the ordination of Father Tolton as a watershed moment for the Catholic Church in America. His ordination showed that the universal Catholic Church considered blacks equal to all others. It also challenged the prevailing opinion that blacks were intellectually and morally inferior. An editorial in 1888 read: "The Catholic Church takes men from all the walks of life and if they but follow her example and teachings she will not only place them beyond the railings, but she will guarantee them a sure footing and endless happiness in the world beyond the grave."[5]

He also championed the work of Mother Katharine Drexel and her religious community who were opening Catholic schools for black and Native American children. People of color were often denied entry into Catholic schools and Rudd defended Mother Katharine against public criticism that she should use her money among her own race.

Like Father Tolton, Rudd received many requests to speak and lecture around the country. Also like Father Tolton, he often spoke about how the Catholic Church was the true liberator of black Americans. Having spoken at several national gatherings of Catholics, the idea began to form in Rudd's mind of a national gathering of black Catholics in Washington, DC. He first proposed the congress in the *American Catholic Tribune* in May 1888. No group was more passionate or desirous of the advancement of black people than black Catholics, he said. For that reason they should gather and become leaven for their race in America, "To have our people realize the Church's extent among them. We are hidden away, as it were. Let us stand forth and look at one another. . . . Every Colored Catholic must, at times, feel that his Colored brethren look upon him as an alien, and may, even be told so. Our Protestant friends have false notions of us," he wrote.[6] When black Catholics gather they will get to know each other in ways that they had not been able to previously. "Gather them and let them exchange views on questions affecting their race; then uniting on a course of action, behind which would stand the majestic Church of Christ, they must inevitably become—what has already been said they should be—the bearer of their race," Rudd wrote.[7] American bishops received an invitation to the congress—even Portland, Maine's Bishop James Healy, the country's first black bishop, although he didn't identify with his African heritage. Healy declined, writing, "My uncertain health hinders me from accepting any invitation to distant places."[8]

Every black parish and black Catholic society was invited to send a delegate to the first "Colored Catholic Congress," which was held January 1–4, 1889, in Washington, DC. Father Tolton celebrated the opening Mass and Baltimore's

Cardinal James Gibbons gave the homily. He told them that Jesus Christ broke down the wall dividing men as evidenced in the multiracial congregation celebrating Mass that day. But he also cautioned them. "Remember the eye of the whole country is upon you. It is not the eye of friendship, but . . . criticism."[9]

During the first congress, participants elected Rudd as president. Newspapers reported around two hundred people attended, although Rudd later listed only eighty names in the *American Catholic Tribune.* At the end of the gathering they drafted a message to all Catholics in America. Participants wrote that they did not know what results of the congress would be other than "an entering wedge in the breaking of the mighty wall of difficulties lifted up for centuries against us and a mere preliminary step in the progressive march and final regeneration of our people."[10] They also pledged themselves to establishing Catholic schools—also trade schools for black men and women—to encouraging temperance among their people; to urging labor unions to admit black men; and to encouraging businesses to hire blacks. They condemned unfair housing practices that relegated blacks to poor, unsafe housing.

Father Tolton served as the congresses' spiritual adviser, often celebrating Mass for the gatherings. In an address during the third congress held in Cincinnati in 1892, he once again proclaimed the Catholic Church the only true liberator of black Americans.

> The Catholic Church deplores double slavery—that of the mind and that of the body. She endeavors to free us of both. I was a poor slave boy but the priests of the Church did not disdain me. It was through the influence of one of them that I became what I am tonight. I must now give praise to that son of the Emerald Isle, Father Peter McGirr, who

promised me that I would be educated and he kept his word. It was the priests of the Church who taught me to pray and to forgive my persecutors. When I was admitted to the College of Propaganda I found out that I was not the only black man there. There were students from Africa, China, Japan and other parts of the world. The Church which knows and makes no distinction in race and color had called them all. When the Church does this, is she not a true liberator of the race? She has colored saints—St. Augustine, St. Benedict, St. Monica. She is the Church for our people.[11]

In all, five congresses took place in different cities: 1889 in Washington, DC; 1890 in Cincinnati; 1892 in Philadelphia; 1893 in Chicago; and 1894 in Baltimore. The next National Black Catholic Congress would not be held until 1987. It is unclear why the congresses ended. Historians speculate that the leaders became too militant or perhaps Rome became concerned about the emergence of an active laity percolating in America. Whatever the reason, black Catholic historian and Benedictine Father Cyprian Davis says the congresses were successful because they accomplished Rudd's primary goal. "They demonstrated beyond a doubt not only that a black Catholic community existed but that it was active, devoted, articulate and proud. It also demonstrated that given the opportunity, there was real leadership within the black Catholic community."[12] From the early days, black laypeople had to take the lead in their community because of a lack of black priests. That remains the norm today. The congress drew out lay leaders and also laid the foundation for future lay movements among the people.

In 1894, Rudd moved his offices of the struggling *American Catholic Tribune* to Detroit but no more issues were published. Eventually, although it is unclear when, Rudd moved south to Mississippi where he appeared in the US Census of 1910. By this time he was in his fifties and worked as a lumber mill manager. Soon after he befriended Arkansas's first black millionaire, Scott Bond, and went to work for him. "Over time, and again Rudd must have experienced seasons of disappointment as he watched Jim Crow become more ensconced across the nation," his biographer Gary B. Agee writes. "In the early decades of the twentieth century, it is difficult to find evidence to merit Rudd's faith in the church's commitment to equality and racial justice. Instead the church seems to have in many cases, acquiesced to Jim Crow culture as did other Christian denominational groups."[13]

Rudd suffered a stroke in 1932 and did not recover. He died on December 3, 1933. He was seventy-nine.

CHAPTER NINE

On to Chicago

The relationship between the Catholic faith and city of Chicago dates all the way back to the first Europeans arriving there in September 1673. French Jesuit Father Jacques Marquette and his exploration team brought their boats to the portage between the Des Plaines and Chicago rivers. Chicago's first permanent, non-Native American settler was the black Catholic Jean Baptiste Point de Sable, "a French-speaking mulatto with an Indian wife."[1] He probably hailed from Montreal, Canada, and was a freeman. De Sable and his wife, Catherine, established a farm in the area.

In 1833, the town of Chicago was incorporated and that same year a group of French, Irish, and British Catholics petitioned Bishop Joseph Rosati of St. Louis, whose diocese included most of the Midwest, for a priest to minister to them. Most of Chicago's residents were Catholics, many with Native American blood or who were married to Native Americans. That community established the parish of St. Mary in May 1833. In 1843, Chicago became its own diocese and included the entire state of Illinois. Irishman Bishop William Quarter was appointed its first shepherd. In 1880,

Chicago became an archdiocese, which made it preeminent over the other dioceses in Illinois. The bishop then became an archbishop. In 1853 the Diocese of Quincy was created, followed by Alton (later Springfield) in 1857.

Blacks were also in Chicago, dating back to the early 1700s as slaves for the French. Illinois joined the Union as a free state in 1818 but strict state laws called Black Codes forbade black residents from voting, from bringing legal suits against whites, and from owning or bearing arms. The state repealed these laws at the end of the Civil War in 1865. Following the Civil War and the migration of free blacks to northern cities, a divide grew in segments of the black community. Prosperous free blacks living in the cities before the Civil War did not want to be pulled down by the freed people, thinking them uneducated, uncouth, and threatening to their standing in society.

A few years after the Civil War, on October 8, 1871, most of Chicago burned to the ground in what was known as the Great Chicago Fire. The Midwest was in the middle of a drought and many of the city's buildings were made out of wood. While the fire began in Mrs. Catherine O'Leary's barn, her much-maligned cow did not start it. The cause is unknown but the fire quickly spread through much of downtown, killing nearly three hundred people. Ninety thousand lost their homes and 17,450 buildings were destroyed, with damages totaling $200 million.[2] The Catholic Church itself suffered nearly $1 million in property loss in the conflagration. But the city quickly rebuilt and out of the ashes the concept of a skyscraper was born, using the sturdier materials brick and steel. A second large fire in 1874 displaced many middle-class members of the black population, which is when the more segregated sections of the city started to form.

When Father Tolton arrived in Chicago, the black population was around twenty-seven thousand out of around one million people and was very segregated in an area south of downtown's business district called the Black Belt. Later the neighborhood came to be called Bronzeville for the skin color of its residents.[3] Most were Protestant and Evangelicals. Those who could find work did so as personal servants in private homes and in hotels and restaurants, earning an average of five to thirty dollars a week. The majority of Chicago's black population was made up of women, children, the elderly, and the sick. Many were also jobless.

In 1893, the city played host to the World's Columbian Exposition, also known as the World's Fair, commemorating the four hundredth anniversary of Christopher Columbus landing in the New World. Father Tolton was ministering to Chicago's black community during the time and may have even visited the fair. Organizers set out to wow the world with its "White City"[4] of pavilions created especially for the fair that showcased American achievements and those of other countries. Even though the fair took place thirty years after the historic end of slavery, black Americans were left out of the planning and their story was as well. Yet they could work at the fair as performers, speakers, security, and in other low-level positions. One stall featured ready-made pancake mix promoted by a character named Aunt Jemima, a large, black woman and a caricature of plantation cooks that denigrated the black community. Responding to exclusion from the fair's planning and programming, leading black Americans drafted the pamphlet, "The Reason Why the Colored American Is Not in the World's Columbian Exposition," which highlighted achievements by the community and was circulated during the event. Contributing to it were prominent journalist Ida B. Wells and former slave and abolitionist Frederick Douglass.

Runaway slaves and freed men and women established Chicago's first black Catholic community in the 1840s. But it was not until 1881 when some type of official parish formed. Father Joseph Rowles, pastor of St. Mary Parish, on Ninth and Wabash streets just south of the city's business center, and on the edge of the segregated neighborhood for blacks, reached out to black Catholics and with them started the St. Augustine Society, named after the great African saint and bishop. Many of these members moved to the city from areas in the South that were historically Catholic and where they would have been educated in the faith. Father Rowles celebrated Mass for this society and they reached out to other blacks about the message of the church. Black Catholics celebrated Mass in the basement of St. Mary for seven years. This sub-parish was dependent on St. Mary's for financial support.

While many were poor themselves, members of the St. Augustine Society managed a "common fund" to which all contributed and that was supplemented by donations from white friends that allowed the society to help the poor, visit the sick, and bury the dead among their people. For everything else they relied upon St. Mary's for support. Worshippers were a mix of those barred from other Catholic churches in the city, some people from other denominations who were recipients of the society's charity, and newcomers from the South coming to the city for jobs. These black Catholics, like their counterparts around the country, were anxious to have their own pastor.

A year after Father Tolton's ordination they approached Archbishop Patrick Feehan, asking that he try to have the country's first black priest transferred to Chicago. Eventually Archbishop Feehan succeeded. At the end of 1889, Father Tolton boarded the train for Chicago, some three hundred miles northeast of Quincy. He began his Chicago ministry in the all-purpose basement of St. Mary's Church. When he reported to Archbishop Feehan, Father Tolton was appointed pastor of St. Augustine with full jurisdiction over all black Catholics in Chicago. Unsure of his lodgings, Father Tolton left his mother and his sister Anne in Quincy for the time. One of his first tasks was to plan the building of a church because the community was eager to have its own space and St. Mary's was in sore need of the basement space for other parish activities. Father Tolton found a one-room apartment at 2251 S. Indiana Avenue in a run-down neighborhood. Not long after, he secured a rectory at 448 36th Street and opened a storefront church that he called St. Monica Chapel, after the mother of St. Augustine. At this point he was finally able to fulfill his promise to his mother and sister to bring them to Chicago.

Appeals for Father Tolton to lecture and visit black Catholics around the country did not decrease with his move to Chicago. The "world's most conspicuous man" accepted some of the invitations, mainly as a way to raise money for his new parish, St. Monica. In a letter to Josephite Father John Slattery, rector of St. Joseph Seminary for Colored Missions in Baltimore, he wished for "27 Father Toltons or colored priests"[5] who could meet the number of requests from around the country to visit and lecture. It would have been "a grand thing," he said, to be a traveling missionary ministering to black Catholics around the country. That was not where God placed him, however. Instead he was focused on the 270 souls from 400 families in Chicago. He wrote of turning down a lecture in St. Paul, Minnesota, because he was trying to gather more people for his parish "for these poor people here who had been left in a bag with both ends open if I must say it and the Irish bishop has given them all up to me."[6] He also told Father Slattery that he would no longer tolerate jealousy from his brother priests like he did in Quincy. If a similar situation arose, Father Tolton wrote, he would pack up and head to the Josephites in Baltimore. For the most part he seemed to feel safe in Chicago.

The fact that he was living in poverty with his people, did not receive a salary, and rarely had a break because there were so many people who needed his help was noted in a letter from Mary C. Elmore to Father Slattery. Despite all of the positive press Father Tolton received in the Josephites' magazine and in the *American Catholic Tribune*, "he is left to struggle on almost alone; in poverty and humility, grappling with the giant task of founding a church and congregation in Chicago," she wrote.[7] His ardent charity and self-denying zeal was ever apparent and an inspiring witness to others. Everyone felt blessed to be in his presence, Elmore wrote.

Just before Father Tolton's arrival in Chicago, Rudd's *American Catholic Tribune* hired Captain Lincoln C. Valle as its Chicago correspondent. While Father Tolton's moves were often chronicled in this newspaper, the whole of his Chicago community was also featured in these pages upon his arrival. Valle became one of Father Tolton's friends, a close collaborator, and an outspoken champion of black Catholics in the city. During the celebration of Archbishop Feehan's silver jubilee in 1891, it was Valle who delivered a public address on behalf of "Negro Catholics." He too proclaimed the Catholic Church as the only entity blind to race in its history, the true liberator of blacks. He also called on fellow Catholics to unite with them to "lift up" the millions of black people in the United States. Valle addressed the often-prevailing prejudice that claimed blacks as a race were unable to be educated. "The question is often asked, is the negro susceptible of education? Yes, answer the statistics. In the Southern States, in 1865, among one thousand negroes you could find one that knew the alphabet, whilst to-day, more than twenty-per cent [*sic*] of all over ten years old can read and write. This proportion is so much the more to be remarked as there are many illiterate whites in those States," Valle said. "More might be said on this question, but suffice it to say that we, the Negro Catholics of Chicago, will show good examples of sobriety and charity to all men, for no sermon is as powerful as the unspoken sermon of good example preached by a model, Christian man."[8]

Valle interviewed Father Tolton in the *American Catholic Tribune* a little over one year after the priest's arrival in Chicago. Father Tolton shared the hurdles he faced and continued to face in ministering to the black Catholic community: "I began my mission on the 29th of November 1889, under many difficulties. At first the Colored people were scattered, having no special shepherd, they were fast drifting into Protestantism. No one can really imagine the heart of a young priest, going into a strange city seeking those of his own faith who have become cool and indifferent," Father Tolton told Valle.[9]

With about twenty committed people, Father Tolton took over services in St. Mary's basement. After just four months, two hundred people were regularly attending Mass and were committed to building their own church. While he began working on that prospect upon his arrival in Chicago, white people who donated to the fund in the past questioned where the money was going. White friends of the parish were asking, "How long will you be building up your church? These Colored people have been begging for nine years and no church yet. What has become of all the money collected for that purpose?" Father Tolton said. "I had a bank note of $1,419 to show them. By that means they see that the Colored Catholics were accumulating that amount nine years; but how can property be bought and a church built with so small an amount? When property in Chicago, as everybody knows, is not low. With that small amount I began to purchase property amounting to $9,000."[10] Support from Archbishop Feehan and "three Irish ladies" buoyed Father Tolton, but other white Catholics refused to donate until the cornerstone was laid. "As to collections, I have not received one cent. Still the question arises, 'What is Father Tolton doing? He surely receives a share of that collection?' Had I, I would have begun my church ere [*sic*] this hour. His Grace, the Archbishop, intends to look into the matter."

To keep the payments up on the property, he arranged fairs and other events and tried to keep the people encouraged. He questioned mandated collections for the church overseas when so much support was needed at home. That charity should include sending black men to seminary to become priests for the community, he said. "How do we expect for them to study if they are not brought up in the faith? How can they be brought into the faith if the priest has no means nor ways to bring them into the faith? How can we bring them into the faith without a suitable place and how can we have a suitable place without the necessary assistance? Let us remember that colleges must depend upon the priests in the missions for its aspirants and they ought to be encouraged in every possible way," Father Tolton told Valle. "I am alone and am sorry for it for the more Colored priests we have, the more sure we are gaining over a great number of our people since they have said to me, 'Father Tolton, I think it is glorious for us to have a priest of our own nationality. Since we can approach them with confidence knowing they will not give us hard feelings.' "[11]

Father Tolton also told Valle that people regularly asked him why he didn't go to a diocese in the South to minister.

His answer was first, the Propaganda Fide sent him to Quincy and then he was called to Chicago. "If I save 500 of these souls in this city I will say 'Now dismiss thy servant, O Lord.'" Father Tolton felt pressured from all sides, as often happens to those blazing a path in history. Not only did he receive pressure to build a church, missions and priests that he turned down for speaking engagements felt slighted and told him he was disappointing his people. They did not consider that he turned down engagements to serve his congregation.

> By my refusal I received strong replies, then my conscience told me to remain at home, through fear that my own little flock would be scattered, hence these are my reasons for not appearing in the 39 places that desire me at this present time. O! How grand it would be to have 39 Colored Priests to go to those places and sow the good seed of the word of God in the hearts of those dear Colored people. The harvest is great, the workers few and far between. I can determine as far as I am able to collect many aspirants for the Priest-hood, for I have the salvation of my people at heart.

CHAPTER TEN

Fellow Pioneer, Mother Katharine Drexel

Among the leading historical figures of Father Tolton's time in the area of religion and race was Mother Katharine Drexel.

Katharine Drexel, who became the second American-born saint, was one of three daughters born to Francis Drexel, a well-known millionaire banker in Philadelphia. Himself a generous philanthropist, he and his family were faith-filled Catholics with hearts for service.

In 1887 and 1888, Katharine and her sisters traveled to Native American reservations in the west along with Monsignor Joseph Stephan, director of the Catholic Indian Missions Bureau, which was established after the Third Plenary Council of Baltimore. She was so moved by their plight that during a private audience in 1887 she personally appealed to Pope Leo XIII to send a missionary priest to minister to them. The pope turned the question around and asked her why she herself could not become a missionary to this group of people. Katharine also shared with him that she felt a calling to religious life as a contemplative. The pope reportedly told her to focus her religious vocation outward and with the Native Americans. She began using her wealth to build schools on the reservations. She also started supporting black missions.

Her father, who died in 1885, left each of his three daughters large inheritances. At the same time, he wrote the terms of the inheritances so that if none of his daughters had children, the money would be divided up among a group of charities. Katharine never challenged her father's will so the income supporting all of the missions and her religious sisters ended upon her death.

At the encouragement and guidance of family friend Bishop James O'Conner of Omaha, Nebraska, Katharine founded the Sisters of the Blessed Sacrament in Bensalem, Pennsylvania, whose ministry it was to work with black and Native American missions. She spent her novitiate with the Sisters of Mercy in Pittsburgh, Pennsylvania. Taking the name Mary Katharine, she professed vows on February 12, 1891, becoming the first member of her order. At that time 134 communities of women religious existed in the United States. When she died there were 343. Many did not last but the Sisters of the Blessed Sacrament remain active today.

Becoming a nun was a risky venture during Katharine's time. In addition to targeting and terrorizing black Americans, the Ku Klux Klan also persecuted Catholics, Jews, and non-Americans. At one point the Klan burned a cross on the grounds of the motherhouse in Bensalem.[1] There was also virulent anti-Catholicism going on at the time, directed in large part toward the huge influx of European immigrants. Between 1860 and 1895 the Catholic population increased fourfold, which upset the largely Protestant nation.

For some time, all of her religious sisters were white. This was a deliberate decision on Katharine's part because she did not want to be seen as competing with communities of black religious women that existed at the time. The first black woman wouldn't enter the community until 1955. During Mother Katharine's lifetime she founded almost sixty missions and schools for Native and black Americans. The first was in Santa Fe, New Mexico, in 1894 for the Pueblo people. In 1917 she established the country's first Catholic university for black people. St. Xavier in New Orleans opened to train black men and women as teachers to teach in segregated schools. People of any faith could attend the university.

The Eucharist was central to her life and she spent many hours—especially in her later life—before the Blessed Sacrament. In 1937 at the age of seventy-eight, Mother Katharine retired from leading her community. She died on March 3, 1955, at ninety-six. St. Pope John Paul II canonized her on October 1, 2000.

Word reached Father Tolton about Mother Katharine's generosity and concern for his people and, during his years in Chicago, he appealed to her generosity for St. Monica's. Three letters from Father Tolton to Mother Katharine exist in the archives of the Blessed Sacrament Sisters. In the first, Father Tolton introduced himself to the heiress and philanthropist. At that time, Katharine was finishing studies with the Mercy Sisters in Pittsburgh prior to establishing her new community. "I am in a new missionary field and nothing to start with," he wrote to her from St. Monica's. "I hope that you will assist us if it is not too much to ask of you, but I suppose all your charity is nearly exhausted by this time as you have helped so many missions." He signed the letter "Tolton (Colored Catholic priest) [*sic*]."[2]

In the second letter, he apologized for "vexing" her with his appeals for support. He also revealed that he felt he was being "watched" by everyone waiting for him to fall or for a chance to make him fall. The Ku Klux Klan persecuted many and hangings took place with terrifying regularity in the South. These times of Reconstruction and post-Reconstruction after the Civil War saw increased tensions among the whites and freed blacks, not just in the South but the North as well. Many in the Union opposed the war—not because they supported abolishing slavery but because they did not want the Union to break apart.

As ever, he tells Mother Katharine, he is moved by her generosity toward his people. "I for one cannot tell how to conduct myself when I see one person at least showing their love for the Colored race. One thing I do know, and that is it took the Catholic Church 100 years here in America to show up such a person as yourself," Father Tolton tells her. "In the whole history of the Church in America we can't find one person that has sworn to lay out their treasury for the sole benefit of the Colored and Indians."[3]

While he stood as the first recognized black priest in America, Mother Katharine stood as the first person to make such a sacrifice for the downtrodden blacks and Native Americans. They both lived in a time when the South was looking on with an "angry eye" and the North was criticizing every act and "watching every move I make," he wrote, adding, "they watch me just the same as the Pharisees did Our Lord—they watched Him."

When his new church was finished, it would create a stir around the United States, Father Tolton wrote, and he would pursue that work as long as God gave him life, "for I see that I have principalities to resist anywhere and everywhere I go. The world is indeed a great book and I have read all of its pages." A notation in this letter indicates that a donation of $100 (which equals a little over $2,000 today) was sent to Father Tolton. Later, once a school for black Catholics opened at St. Monica's, Mother Katharine sent members of her community to staff the school. The archives note that from 1893–1923, Mother Katharine donated $36,750 (the equivalent of around $1 million in 2018) to St. Monica's.

Just two months before he died, Father Tolton wrote one last letter to Mother Katharine and updated her on the work at St. Monica's. In the letter dated May 12, 1897, he said while he had 260 souls to "render account of before God's majesty," altogether there were 500 black Catholics in Chicago but the others "have become like until the dead limbs of a tree and without moisture because no one had taken care of them."

Father Tolton shared with her how he had been summoned recently to the deathbed of a woman who was away from the church for nine years because she "was hurled out of a white church and even cursed at by the Irish members." But on the edge of death she called for Father Tolton to receive last rites. He thanked God that she had a black priest to send for. It was not just black Catholics who called him their own. "These dear people feel proud that they have one to look after them. Even Protestants when sick will send for me in preference to their preachers and treat me with the greatest respect not one is prejudiced at all that makes me feel like there is a great work for me."[4]

CHAPTER ELEVEN

St. Monica's Becomes a Reality

Parish life continued at St. Monica's and in 1891, after a $10,000 pledge from Mrs. Annie O'Neill, Archbishop Feehan gave the go-ahead to start plans for a church for black Catholics. Fund-raising stepped up with the archbishop himself donating $1,000. The groundbreaking was held in August 1892. The *Chicago Daily Tribune* reported on the news in January 1893. In the same story was news of a new church for St. Boniface Parish, then located at Noble and Cornell streets. The congregation of over six thousand had outgrown its space so the church purchased twenty lots for $90,000. At that date the parish had raised over $200,000 ($5.4 million in 2018) for the new building in comparison to the $10,000 raised for St. Monica's and its smaller $36,000 price tag. "Rev. Father Tolton is working every scheme possible to pay off the debt property. He says that if he was as well known in Chicago as he is in Quincy, Ill., the people would build his church at once. In Quincy he has just to step off the train at the depot," newspapers reported.

It was not easygoing. The September 16, 1893, issue of *The New World*, the newspaper for the Archdiocese of Chicago, reported that while the church foundation had been laid, "we regret to say that with few exceptions, the Catholics of Chicago have not been as generous to this enterprise as its merits deserve. Father Tolton has succeeded in collecting enough cash and securing promises to justify him in beginning the work of construction, but he will need much money before the building now begun can be completed," they wrote. "He has been in Chicago nearly four years, laboring zealously and almost exclusively at this work. His patience and perseverance have been admirable but he has always been supported by his hope that the Catholics of Chicago would at last enable him to erect a church for his people, to keep those of them who are Catholics in the faith, and to attract to the faith the thousands who have no religion of any kind. We sincerely hope that in the future Father Tolton's efforts will find more encouragement and practical support than in the past."

A December 3, 1893, article in the *Chicago Daily Tribune* revealed the proposed church design. St. Monica's would be the first black church west of Baltimore and, in keeping with its noble history, was designed by the black architect G. W. Brown from the firm Brown and Higginbotham. "The building will make a very imposing appearance," the newspaper reported. Designed in Gothic style, the walls would be made of pressed brick with trimmings of Bedford stone. Two windows of "cathedral glass" would be installed over the entrance. Two large towers would flank the building, one of which could be made into a bell tower. Seven rooms for catechism classes were planned for the ground floor. If needed, the walls could open to create one large room with seating for 500. The sanctuary would be on the main church floor with seating for 850. Three hundred more could sit in the gallery above. A pipe organ would be installed in the gallery. "On the ground floor will be the pastor's study and library. The interior finish will be of white oak and later on the walls will be elaborately decorated. The building will be heated with steam and lighted by electricity. The roof will be of tile," the *Chicago Daily Tribune* reported.

Construction halted that winter and a temporary roof was put on the completed first level of the church. An official dedication ceremony took place January 15, 1894. Regular Sunday Masses began immediately. "It is the first Catholic church in this city to be built by colored people. More than this, it is the first church of the kind constructed in this State and probably the only Catholic church in the West that has been built by colored members of that faith for their own use," the *Chicago Daily Tribune* reported. Work was expected to be finished on July 15, 1894, just eleven months from its start. The priest told the newspaper he estimated that eight hundred black Catholics lived in the city and he expected Mass attendance to increase now that there was a church. Unbeknownst to Father Tolton, his dream of St. Monica's church would never be realized because of lack of funds and other support.

While work went on for their own church, Father Tolton continued with his daily ministry of teaching the faith, offering Mass, spending countless hours in the confessional, and traversing the city to meet with his people. Often he invited church groups to meet in the apartment where he lived with his mother. His fellow blacks were often poor and in need of much help. He did what he could, appealing to the charitable institutions at the time for much-needed items like food and clothing. "Mother Tolton" continued to live with her son and serve as sacristan for the church. Since people continued calling her "Mother" it is likely she was the matriarch of St. Monica's, someone sought for advice, guidance, and help—a spiritual mother. Even given her son's notoriety there was still not much reported about her life— just brief mentions like a note in the *American Catholic Tribune* among a list of goings-on in the local community, as was the custom in those days: "Mrs. Martha Tolton, Mother of the Rev. Father Tolton, has been ill but safe to say she is convalescent."

Despite all that he had going on, Father Tolton continued to make strides with his people and helped them see their value as children of God. For example, he and Lincoln Valle petitioned Archbishop Feehan to establish a chapter of the Ladies Catholic Benevolent Association at the parish. Founded in 1890, the mission of the Ladies Catholic Benevolent Society is to provide financial support to women who encounter losses in their lives that make them vulnerable. St. Monica's established the society's first black chapter. For its first meeting, Father Tolton gathered at his home "ladies who shrink not from storms nor tempests, ladies who are not afraid of coming when requested to do so." These women were leaders in the church community.

Father Tolton, it seems, held a progressive view on women. Perhaps it came from his close relationship with his mother. His view was evident in a lecture on women he gave at the parish that was reported on by the *American Catholic Tribune* (April 11, 1891). The lecture, titled "What is Woman," required a donation of twenty-five cents to benefit the Ladies Catholic Benevolent Society. "Father Tolton began by giving a resume of the Biblical account of women and their work for and in the church. He dwelt upon the conspicuous manner in which the Saviour had blest [sic] woman and how the faith of woman had kept her close to Him even when he was deserted by man," the newspaper recounted. Father

Tolton said women were no longer considered "mere chattel." In the nineteenth century, he noted, men no longer viewed women as Adam did Eve—the cause of their sorrow and sin—but rather the source of their spiritual enlightenment. "When men have come into the full cognizance of the divine plan of creation, woman shall stand by his side as his acknowledged equal, mentally and morally, and spiritually his superior," he reportedly said.

Despite his regular duties, at the back of his mind was always the finances of St. Monica's and the money needed to complete construction on the church. For that he had to court donors, often wealthy whites in Chicago sympathetic to the plight of the black community. He also continued occasional travel to earn money for his parish. On January 31, 1891, the *American Catholic Tribune* published a story about a lecture he gave in Janesville, Wisconsin. An estimated one thousand people filled St. Patrick Church to hear him speak on his favorite topic, "The Catholic Church Teaches All Nations, No Color Line There."

"The speaker opened his discourse with the statement that he came before his audience with an assertion which would not require the least proof whatever if all men of this enlightened age of ours were of one mind regarding the lawful claims of the Catholic church or would even come to the conclusion that she is the true church of Christ." The Catholic Church has all nations in her fold and has always been, "the true teacher, true emancipator of the colored race," he said. Jesus died for all races and classes wrapped up in sin. "We should all go to that church in which the Negro problem is not discussed since it teaches that all men are equal in the sight of the Almighty. The speaker illustrated this point with examples which had come under his personal observation while studying at Rome," the newspaper reported.

Chicago newspapers also took note of Father Tolton's presence in the city. On November 19, 1893, the *Chicago Daily Tribune* published a story on clergy who ministered to the city's black congregations. While several men were featured, Father Tolton received the most praise. "There is no more interesting figure in the life of our city than Father Augustus Tolton, the rector of St. Monica's Roman Catholic Church now in the course of erection at the corner of Dearborn and Thirty-sixth streets. This great, kindly-faced man is now well known as the first Catholic priest of the American negro family. Father Tolton is a remarkable character," the article said. "Father Tolton has all of the fervency and emotional ardor of his race. There is a warmth, a temper of the tropics, a lingering echo of the ecstasy and pathos which glimmered through the mists of darker days that possess his personality with a fascinating and all-pervading charm."

All the while, Father Tolton continued encouraging and, when he could, financially supporting vocations to the priesthood among black men. He wrote of his efforts to Father Joseph Slattery at the Josephite seminary in Baltimore. The letter was sent to acknowledge the Josephites' ordaining of P. J. Griffin, a black American, to subdeacon. Father Tolton had directed Griffin to the community. "Deo Gratias I will exclaim, now dear father, I will send you another one if you say so under the name of Mr. T. P. Watterfield of Hamilton, Ill. More than that dear father Slattery all that I know or hear of I will direct them to you for you are the only priest that cares for us anyhow," Father Tolton wrote. "After I start my New Church I will devote a great deal of my time to that college for I intend to get a house of aspirants for the priesthood right from this city. I have one right now and I am instructing him."[1]

Again he says that if Archbishop Feehan had not invited him to Chicago he would have joined the Josephites to escape the persecution he faced by Father Weis in Quincy. He stopped short of detailing his persecutions because he said he did not want to endanger the church's mission to blacks in America. "I shall advise every young colored aspirant to join that order so as to have direct protection at home without having to send a letter to Rome and then wait 6 months or more for an answer in case anything transpires through the jealousy of a brother priest that is the cause of my being in Chicago now—through the jealousy of a Dutch [*sic*] priest which facts I have kept hid and will never let them out through fear of it greatly injuring the success of the mission among the colored race."

While he had friends among whites, Father Tolton still lived in the reality that wherever he went he was judged by the color of his skin. Most of the time he didn't speak publicly about this, but on one notable occasion he did. In March 1893, Father Peter McGirr, who helped Father Tolton find his vocation to the priesthood, died. While the trip to Quincy for the funeral would no doubt be a solemn one for the priest, it also came with an incident of prejudice when he and his friend Lincoln Valle arrived and were denied rooms at the Tremont House.

The incident created such a public stir that Father Tolton wrote a letter to the editor of the *Quincy Daily Journal* explaining what happened. "Those who know me know that I am not an alarmist, nor am I a person who makes notoriety at anybody's expense. I simply want, through the force of my own character, to prove a different spirit of the people of Quincy, than what was practiced upon me and my friend, Mr. Valle, Monday evening," he began the letter.[2] Father Tolton was invited to attend Father McGirr's funeral. When they arrived in the city, those who organized the funeral met them at the train and took them to Tremont House where all the priests coming for the funeral were staying. When Father Tolton tried to check into rooms for both himself and Valle, he was told no rooms were available and that they should walk around the city for a few hours and return to see if some became available. It was around 11 p.m. at night. "If no one left we would, in order to retire, have to seek other quarters at that time of night. The reader will see the flaws in that excuse," Father Tolton wrote. "I know that on other occasions this kind of refusal has happened from that same house. I thought, however, time and association had worn off the ragged edges of some of these prejudiced and narrow-minded people." He said he spoke so strongly because, on a whole, the people of Quincy accepted him and the committee who organized Father McGirr's funeral and the accommodations for the priests had too much respect for him not to have booked him rooms in advance. While some in Quincy might consider what happened a trivial matter, Father Tolton wrote that he did not. "I feel it is an insult to the millions of true and loyal Americans whom I have the honor to represent."

The newspaper interviewed the owners of the Tremont House—Misters Fletcher and Slocum—and they denied that Father Tolton and Valle were turned away because of their race. No policy against "Negros" existed at the hotel, they told the newspaper. "They say that their books will show that they have repeatedly entertained negros . . . They state positively that they have never yet turned away a respectable and well-behaved negro who has applied to them, when they had a room for him to occupy." Father Tolton did not have a history of confrontation in the face of prejudice. He had a lifetime of facing disparaging comments and maltreatment at the hands of whites but rarely challenged offenses publicly. In this case he did.

The summer before Father Tolton died, Monsignor Theodore Warning from Dubuque, Iowa, stayed with him and Martha Tolton in their house on Chicago's South Side. The priest was taking a summer course at the University of Chicago, located a few miles away. In a letter Monsignor Warning related that they lived in a poorly furnished but very clean house. Meals were simple. They sat around a small table covered with an oil cloth with a kerosene lamp in the middle. "On the wall directly behind Father's place hung a large black rosary. As soon as the evening meal was over, Father Tolton would rise and take the beads from the nail. He kissed the large crucifix reverently," Warning wrote. "We all knelt on the bare floor while the Negro priest in a low voice, led the prayers with deliberate slowness and with unmistakable fervor."[3]

During that time, life for black Americans became less free. In 1896, a year before Father Tolton died, the US Supreme Court handed down its decision on Plessy v. Ferguson, making racial segregation—"separate but equal"—the law of the land. The case originated in Louisiana where a Jim Crow law mandated that railroad cars provide separate accommodations for blacks and whites. The case stemmed from an incident in 1892 when Homer Plessy refused to sit in a segregated car, was arrested, and brought before Judge John Ferguson in New Orleans who upheld the law. The law was challenged in the US Supreme Court on the grounds that it violated the Thirteenth and Fourteenth amendments. The Thirteenth Amendment outlawed slavery and the Fourteenth Amendment granted all citizens, which included former slaves, equal protection under the law. Both of these amendments came out of the Civil War and Reconstruction.

CHAPTER TWELVE

Final Days of Father Tolton and St. Monica's

By the late 1890s, it was clear through comments from people in letters that Father Tolton was working himself to exhaustion. Blacks did not have access to adequate health care and, based on what can be deduced of his personality, Father Tolton put his needs last and answered every call he could for prayer and assistance. Ministering to the poor and the sick, he was often exposed to illness. He was in his early forties but seemed much older. At times Father Tolton delivered his sermons while seated because he didn't have the strength to stand. His hand shook while giving Communion. A story in the Archdiocese of Chicago's newspaper, *The New World*, from June 15, 1895, noted that Father Tolton took a short leave of absence because of his health.

In early July 1897, he set out by train for a priests' retreat at St. Viator College in Bourbonnais, Illinois, located about sixty miles southwest of Chicago. Father Tolton arrived back in Chicago on July 9 in the middle of a massive heat wave. It was 105 degrees that day. Dozens would die that summer from the heat, including a Father Groenbaum of St. Nicholas Parish in Evanston.[1]

Father Tolton got off the train on the South Side near 35th Street and Lake Michigan. It was about ten city blocks from the station to his home. He planned to visit some parishioners along the way, but just a few blocks from the station Father Tolton collapsed on the sidewalk at 36th Street and Ellis Avenue. Several people nearby came to his aid and pulled him under a tree for some shade. They alerted a passing police patrol, which then rushed him to Mercy Hospital located about two miles away. Despite medical attention, his fever increased and he was given the sacrament of extreme unction, or last rites. His mother and sister were by his side along with the Mercy Sisters and the hospital chaplain as he died that evening, July 9, 1897. He was forty-three years old.

The following day the casket bearing his body arrived at St. Monica's. As was customary for caskets bearing people of position or people who were well known, the casket was made of wood and had a glass top so mourners could see the body. Father Tolton's body was dressed in his vestments; a rosary around his hand and a large crucifix were buried with him. A wake was held at the church that day and culminated in a funeral Mass attended by more than one hundred priests. The archdiocese's vicar-general who was second to the archbishop, preached at the funeral. More than one thousand people came to pay their respects to the priest over the two days.

It was Father Tolton's desire to be buried in Quincy, so following the funeral a horse-drawn carriage took his casket to the train where his body was transported back to the town where he grew up. His mother and sister accompanied the body along with Lincoln Valle, some of St. Monica's parishioners, and his spiritual director Father J. Brecks. When they arrived in Quincy the morning of July 13, twelve priests met the body and accompanied it to St. Peter Church where it was placed at the head of the center aisle.

Crowds of both blacks and whites filled the church and overflowed out into the street. Flowers filled the sanctuary. Quincy newspapers reported that "there was seldom such a large funeral." Following Mass, a procession four blocks long accompanied Father Tolton's remains to the cemetery. Some walked while others took carriages or streetcars to the small parish cemetery where his body was interred.

While Father Tolton wished to be buried in St. Peter Cemetery, he did not have a plot there. It is believed that Father Peter Kerr, who celebrated Father Tolton's funeral and was pastor of St. Peter's at the time, gave him his own plot. Father Kerr was later buried in an adjacent plot. Some years later, a gravestone with a large cross was erected to identify their resting places. Father Tolton's inscription is on the east side of the stone and Father Kerr's on the west. Father Tolton's remains actually reside directly in the ground in front of Father Kerr's inscription, as was confirmed during exhumation of his remains in 2016. (See Appendix 2)

The Chicago delegation returned to the city to face the future without its beloved priest. Martha Tolton went to live with her daughter Anne, her husband William Pettis, and their daughter Rosa. Anne died in 1910. Martha continued serving at St. Monica's until her own death in November 1911. News reports listed her age as eighty-five. Martha, Anne, and Anne's family are all buried together at Mount Olivet Cemetery, which is located about twelve miles southwest of where St. Monica's was located, and in a historically Irish part of Chicago. Notably, they aren't buried in any of the cemeteries traditionally reserved for blacks at the time. It is speculated that a descendent of the Pettises later gathered the remains and interred them at Mount Olivet.

Following Father Tolton's death, Archbishop Feehan made St. Monica's a mission served by St. Elizabeth Parish, with only one Mass on Sundays. The congregation began to break up. Valle appealed to Archbishop Feehan to give them a pastor. Lincoln Valle also wrote to Father Slattery with the Josephites, asking him to send Father Charles Uncles, America's second identified black priest. A few years later, Valle himself would leave Chicago and go north to Milwaukee, Wisconsin. In 1908, he and his wife Julia organized black Catholics there into that diocese's first black Catholic parish, St. Benedict the Moor.[2]

Father John Morris was eventually assigned to St. Monica's and served for fifteen years. During his tenure a school for black children opened and Mother Katharine Drexel sent her sisters to run it. Eventually that school merged with St. Elizabeth's school. Construction on St. Monica's church building remained incomplete. In 1917, Archbishop George Mundelein transferred Father Morris to another parish and asked priests from the Society of the Divine Word to take over at St. Monica's. In a move that, intentional or not, harkened back to Father Tolton's days in Quincy, Archbishop Mundelein decreed that only blacks could worship at St. Monica's. Four hundred black families were worshipping at the church. It is unclear how many whites also attended services there.

Archbishop Mundelein, who would later become the archdiocese's first-ever cardinal and America's preeminent Catholic leader, said he was not excluding blacks from worshipping at white churches—especially if they did not live on the South Side where St. Monica's was located— just that whites were not to worship at St. Monica's. This was outlined in a detailed letter to the Divine Word fathers that was published in the archdiocese's newspaper on December 2, 1917. Archbishop Mundelein gave three reasons for his decision: (1) two larger parishes located near St. Monica's were well able to meet the needs of white Catholics; (2) St. Monica's church building was small and unfinished and non-blacks "are crowding, incommoding and embarrassing those for whom the mission was built"; (3) while the parish had looked outside for financial support, blacks now received better wages and should support themselves without assistance. Archbishop Mundelein wrote:

> It would be puerile for us to ignore the fact that a distinction as to color enters very often into the daily happenings of our city. I am not going to argue as to the reasons for or against this line of distinction which causes so much bitterness, nor will I say anything as to the justice or injustice of it. It is sufficient to say that it does exist and I am convinced that I am quite powerless to change it, for I believe the underlying reasons to be more economic than social. What I am concerned about is that my colored children shall not feel uncomfortable in the Catholic Church.

The archbishop hoped that black Catholics could complete construction on St. Monica's and build it into a thriving parish that one day their children's children would look upon with pride. While Archbishop Mundelein's words do not seem meant to demean, they are filled with the prevailing opinion of American whites at that time that blacks were separate from them and somehow second-class people. "The Creator seems to have given them a spirit of reverence and religion that is often lacking in other races," Archbishop Mundelein wrote, adding, with a tone of surprise, that the religious women who ministered to them often became strongly attached to their children. He ended the letter by saying that that same Creator is blind to skin color and would judge us all on the last day by the purity of our hearts and the fruits of our labors. The last part seems at odds with the rest of the letter that certainly judges these Catholics by the color of their skin.

In 1924, Archbishop Mundelein, who that same year was elevated to cardinal, merged St. Monica's into St. Elizabeth's and effectively closed the city's first black Catholic parish and the first black parish in the Midwest. About twenty years later, the city tore down the structure to make room for a housing project.

Who knows how much more Father Tolton would have accomplished had he lived longer? For pioneers like him, even though unwilling, the pressures of breaking through barriers can take their toll. What we do know is that his life was one of heroic virtue and he is an important figure in the American Catholic story.

His commitment was to share with anyone who would listen that the Catholic Church is the true liberator.

APPENDIX 1

Key Dates in Father Tolton's Life and in American History

1849

Martha Jane Chisley, Father Tolton's mother, moves to Missouri from Kentucky as a young slave.

Harriet Tubman escapes from slavery, returns to the South, and becomes one of the main "conductors" on the Underground Railroad.

1854

April 1, Augustus is born to Martha Jane Chisley. Father John O'Sullivan, pastor of St. Peter Church in Brush Creek, Missouri, baptizes him on May 29, 1854.

1857

In the Dred Scott case, the US Supreme Court decides that blacks are not US citizens, and that Congress has no power to restrict slavery in any federal territory.

1859
Martha Jane marries fellow slave Peter Paul in Missouri.

1861
Civil War begins with firing on Fort Sumter in South Carolina on April 14.

1863
January 1, President Abraham Lincoln's Emancipation Proclamation legally frees all slaves in the Confederacy.

July–September, Martha Jane flees Missouri with Augustus, Anne, and Charles in tow.

In September, Peter Paul Lefevre enlists in the Union Army, Third Regiment, Arkansas Infantry.

In Quincy, Illinois, at the age of nine, Augustus begins working in a tobacco factory. His brother Charles dies.

1865
Augustus enters St. Boniface School and leaves one month later because the parish and staff were being threatened and harassed by his presence.

Civil War ends on April 26.

1866
Bishops in the United States hold Second Plenary Council of Baltimore to discuss establishing a national ministry to emancipated slaves. At the end of the council, no such resolution was made.

1868

Augustus enrolled in St. Peter School, Quincy, by Father Peter McGirr who was the first to tell Augustus he thought he had a vocation to the priesthood.

The Fourteenth Amendment to the Constitution was ratified on July 21, granting citizenship to any person born or naturalized in the United States.

1870

Augustus is confirmed in St. Peter Church at the age of sixteen and receives his First Communion.

1871

The Great Chicago Fire wipes out much of the city's downtown.

1872

Augustus graduates from St. Peter School. He is eighteen.

1873

Priests begin tutoring Augustus in preparation for the seminary.

1875

James Healy is named bishop of Portland, Maine, becoming the first black bishop in America, although he denied his African heritage.

1878

Augustus is enrolled at St. Francis Solano College in Quincy. Students from Missouri threaten to leave but Franciscans tell them Augustus is staying.

Augustus helps local priests start a ministry to black people in Quincy.

1880
Census reports US population of 50 million. Blacks comprise 6.5 million.

Augustus departs for Rome on February 15 where he will enter Urban College, sponsored by the Propagation of the Faith.

1882
Lower level of St. Mary's Church in Chicago becomes Chicago's first black parish. Mass celebrated there until 1889.

1883
Cardinal Giovanni Simeoni, prefect for the Vatican Congregation for the Propagation of the Faith, calls the archbishops in America to Rome, ordering them to take action on ministry to freed black people.

1884
During the Third Plenary Council of Baltimore, the American bishops institute a national collection to support black and Indian missions; encourage seminarians and religious men and women to work among these peoples.

1886
Father Tolton is ordained a priest in Rome at St. John Lateran Basilica on April 24 and told he would return as a missionary to his home country and to Quincy.

Celebrates his first Mass at St. Peter's Basilica in Rome on April 25.

Celebrates his first Mass on American soil with the Sisters of the Poor of St. Francis in Hoboken, New Jersey, on July 7.

Celebrates his first Mass in Quincy at St. Boniface Church on July 18, and becomes pastor of St. Joseph Church.

1889
First Colored Catholic Congress held in Washington, DC, January 1–4.

Father Tolton begins his ministry in Chicago on December 19.

1891
St. Monica Church opens in a storefront in the 2200 block of South Indiana Avenue.

1893
Chicago hosts the World's Columbian Exposition but black Americans are left out of the organization and their history is ignored. In protest, journalist Ida B. Wells and abolitionist Frederick Douglass help produce the pamphlet "The Reason Why the Colored American Is Not in the World's Columbian Exposition."

1894
Dedication of St. Monica Church on January 14.

1896
Plessy v. Ferguson: US Supreme Court in a vote of seven to one upholds the constitutionality of state laws requiring racial segregation under the doctrine of "separate but equal."

1897

Father Tolton dies at Mercy Hospital in Chicago on July 9. He was forty-three. Funeral at St. Monica Church, 36th and Dearborn Street, on July 12. Funeral at St. Peter Church in Quincy on July 13.

APPENDIX 2

Saint Augustus Tolton?

"Virtue has consequences, and virtue is stronger than evil. History is what God remembers. The rest passes," said Chicago Cardinal Francis George when presiding over a service formally sealing documents related to Father Augustus Tolton's canonization in preparation for them being sent to Rome for the next phase of the process. It was September 29, 2014.[1]

Just a few years earlier in 2011, the cardinal formally opened Father Tolton's cause during the worldwide Year for Priests called for by Pope Benedict XVI. A diocese must appoint various people to lead the cause, such as an episcopal delegate and promoter of justice, as well as theological and historical commissions and a guild. At the head of all of this is the diocesan bishop and the postulator whom he appoints. The Vatican in February 2012 named Tolton a "servant of God," the first stage of the canonization process. Chicago Auxiliary Bishop Joseph Perry, postulator (leader) for the cause, then assembled research on Tolton's life into a dossier that was sealed at a September 2014 ceremony overseen by Cardinal George. The collected evidence

includes everything from newspaper articles to correspon-
dence to eyewitness testimonies. "Everything in the record
of the case demonstrates that we had a saint among us and
we hardly noticed," Bishop Perry said. "Father Tolton leaves
behind a shining example of perseverance."[2]

On the morning of December 10, 2016, in St. Peter Cemetery in Quincy, Illinois, Servant of God Augustus Tolton's
cause for canonization moved one step farther as his remains
were exhumed and verified. While digging up Tolton's grave
may seem like a macabre undertaking and the antithesis of
the prayer "may they rest in peace," it is actually a reverent
and well-thought-out part of church law regarding the remains of holy people.

This goes back to very ancient traditions in the church.
One was to document that the person really existed. Finding
the grave was the telltale sign that the person lived, breathed,
and walked this earth. Also, over time in territories hostile
to Christianity, the remains of holy people were gathered
and kept safe to guard against desecration. In addition, the
church wants to ensure the remains are well preserved. A
third reason the church exhumes remains is to determine if
the body is "incorrupt." In the church's history there are
saints' bodies—like St. Clare of Assisi and St. Pio of Pietrel-
cina—that haven't decomposed and are "incorrupt." The
church views this as a miracle and a sign of holiness.

While Tolton died in Chicago in 1897, he requested to be
buried in Quincy, to which he and his family fled after es-
caping slavery in nearby Missouri and where he returned
to minister after being ordained in Rome. He is buried in
St. Peter's Cemetery in a plot with another Quincy priest.
Prior to the exhumation, cemetery crews from the Archdiocese of Chicago and the Diocese of Springfield—within

which Quincy is geographically located—dug six feet down into the clay-based soil to about four inches above what they believed to be Tolton's grave. They removed dirt from a six- by eleven-foot space. Using sonar, they had already verified the grave's location.

The Catholic Church, through the Vatican Congregation of the Causes of Saints, is very specific about how the process must go. There is a canon (church) law that has to be followed, laying out exactly what has to be done and how it's done to the point that the workers are called together to swear an oath to diligence and professionalism. Canon law also requires that dioceses employ a forensic anthropologist, a medical examiner, and an archaeologist in the process. During the exhumation, they found a wooden coffin crushed by the earth in which Tolton was buried. The casket had a glass top because they found a significant amount of broken glass mixed in with the remains. At the time Tolton died, glass-topped coffins were used for people of position or who were well known.

In addition to the skeletal remains, the crews found other items such as metal handles and wood from the coffin, the corpus from a crucifix buried with him, the corpus from his rosary, and a portion of his Roman priest's collar. The intent of all of this is preserving the remains we have of a possible saint. Every bone or item found is properly preserved, then put into a sealed casket and vault, and returned to the ground until the Vatican makes its decision. For Tolton, the exhumation was slow going with a lot of hand digging with trowels and using soft brushes to unearth the remains to make sure as much as possible was preserved. As the remains were unearthed, the forensic pathologist laid them out on a table in a mortuary bag under which was a new priest's alb. The forensic pathologist pieced the bones together anatomically. In addition to the skull, they found Tolton's femurs, rib bones, vertebrae, collarbones, pelvis, portions of the arm bones, and other smaller bones. The forensic pathologist verified by the skull that the remains were of a black person. By the shape and thickness of bones in the pelvic area, he was able to determine that the remains were from a male in his early forties.

Once all of the remains and artifacts were collected, the process to reinter Tolton began. Priests from Springfield vested the remains with a white Roman chasuble and maniple, amice, and cincture. Tolton's remains were then placed in a new casket bearing a plate that identified him as "Servant of God Augustus Tolton," along with his dates of birth, ordination, and death. A document was placed on top of the remains attesting to the work done that day. Then they wrapped a red ribbon around the casket and secured it with a wax seal of the Diocese of Springfield. The coffin was in turn placed in a burial vault with another inscription. A second vault held the broken glass and coffin parts and both containers were reinterred in the grave. A closing prayer service wrapped up the solemn process. The grave will only be opened again if Tolton is beatified. No relics—pieces of bone or any of the other objects found in the grave—were removed that day. Relics can only be shared if Tolton moves on to the next stage in the canonization process—beatification.

Many positive steps are being taken to declare Father Tolton as a saint. In March 2018, the historical consultants in Rome ruled that the *poisitio* (equivalent to a doctoral dissertation on a person's life) was acceptable and the research on Tolton's life was finished. Upon reviewing Father Tolton's cause, a Vatican committee unanimously voted in February 2019 to present the dossier to the Ordinary Meeting of Cardinals and Archbishops, who determines whether a Decree of Heroic Virtues of the candidate be presented to the pope for approval.[3] The Ordinary Meeting of Cardinals and Archbishops agreed that Father Tolton lived the theological virtues of faith, hope, and charity, and the cardinal virtues of prudence, justice, fortitude, and temperance at a heroic level. Pope Francis signed the decree on June 11, 2019, officially advancing Servant of God Augustus Tolton to Venerable Augustus Tolton.[4]

For more information on the cause, visit www.tolton canonization.org.

Notes

Chapter One:
Flight from Slavery—pages 1–7

1. Document from Historical and Theological Commission for Canonization Cause for Augustus Tolton.

2. U.S. National Archives and Records Administration, "Black Soldiers in the U.S. Military During the Civil War," https://www.archives.gov/education/lessons/blacks-civil-war.

3. U.S. Department of the Interior, National Park Service, "Aboard the Underground Railroad: Dr. Richard Eells House," https://www.nps.gov/nr/travel/underground/il3.htm.

4. John Keilman, "3 abolitionists convicted of aiding slaves among those pardoned by Quinn," *Chicago Tribune*, January 1, 2015, www.chicagotribune.com/news/ct-illinois-underground-railroad-clemency-met-20141231-story.html.

5. Reg Ankrom, "Father Peter McGirr: Patron of 'Father Gus,'" *The Herald-Whig*, July 1, 2012, www.whig.com/story/18925044/father-peter-mcgirr-patron-of-father-gus#.

Chapter Two:
Finding His Vocation—pages 8–14

1. Document from Historical and Theological Commission for Canonization Cause for Augustus Tolton.

2. School Sisters of Notre Dame Archives, Milwaukee, Wisconsin.

3. Augustus Tolton (1854–1897), Archdiocese of Chicago historical record for canonization cause.

4. Archives of the Mill Hill Fathers, London, England.

5. Archives of the Propaganda Fide, Rome, Italy.

6. Archives of the Franciscan Generalate, Rome, Italy.

Chapter Three:
The Catholic Church and Slavery—pages 15–20

1. Pope Gregory XVI, *In Supremo Apostolatus*, December 3, 1839, www.ewtn.com/library/papaldoc/g16sup.htm.

2. James M. O'Toole, *Passing for White: Race, Religion, and the Healy Family, 1820–1920* (Boston: University of Massachusetts Press, 2002), 33.

3. Cyprian Davis, *The History of Black Catholics in the United States* (New York: Crossroad, 1991), 117.

4. Davis, *History of Black Catholics*, 118.

5. Edward J. Misch, "The Catholic Church and the Negro, 1865–1884," July 9, 2006, https://www.tandfonline.com/doi/abs/10.1080/0020486740120609?journalCode=ueee20.

6. Davis, *History of Black Catholics*, 119.

7. Ibid., 132.

8. Ibid., 133.

Chapter Four:
The Healys—pages 21–28

1. O'Toole, *Passing for White*, 31–32.

2. Ibid., 76.

3. Ibid., 115.

4. Ibid., 125.

5. Ibid., 140.

6. Ibid., 142.

7. Georgetown University Library, "Patrick F. Healy, S.J. (1834–1910)," https://repository.library.georgetown.edu/handle/10822/552740.

Chapter Five:
Tolton Goes to Rome—pages 29–38

1. Pontificia Universitas Urbaniana, "The Urbaniana University," http://www.urbaniana.org/en/ateneo/storia.htm.
2. *St. Joseph's Advocate* (January 1888): 322–26.
3. Archives of the Collegium Urbanum, Rome, Italy.
4. Robert F. McNamara, *The American College in Rome, 1855–1955* (New York: Christopher Press, 1956).
5. McNamara, *American College in Rome*, 96.
6. "St. Philip Neri," *Catholic Online*, https://www.catholic.org /saints/saint.php?saint_id=97.
7. McNamara, *American College in Rome*, 101.
8. Ibid., 98–99.
9. Archives of the Propaganda Fide, Rome, Italy.
10. Archives of the Collegium Urbanum, Rome, Italy.
11. Archives, Josephite Fathers, Baltimore, Maryland.
12. Letter to Propaganda Fide from Father Tolton 1886, Archives of the Propaganda Fide, Rome, Italy.

Chapter Six:
Back to Quincy—pages 39–44

1. Archives of the Propaganda Fide, Rome, Italy.
2. Augustus Tolton (1854–1897), Archdiocese of Chicago historical record for canonization cause.
3. *St. Joseph's Advocate* (January 1888).
4. *American Catholic Tribune* (March 1891).

Chapter Seven:
Trouble Begins—pages 45–52

1. Archives of the Propaganda Fide, Rome, Italy.
2. Ibid.
3. Ibid.
4. Ibid.
5. Ibid.
6. Ibid.

Chapter Eight:
His Friend, Daniel Rudd—pages 53–59

1. Gary B. Agee, *Daniel Rudd: Calling a Church to Justice* (Collegeville, MN: Liturgical Press, 2017), 22.

2. Pat McNamara, "Daniel A. Rudd: Black Catholic Journalist and Pioneer," Patheos.com, June 11, 2012, www.patheos.com/catholic /black-catholic-journalist-pat-mcnamara-06-12-2012.

3. *American Catholic Tribune* (January 3 and 10, 1891).

4. Ibid.

5. Agee, *Daniel Rudd*, 37.

6. Davis, *History of Black Catholics*, 171.

7. Ibid., 172.

8. O'Toole, *Passing for White*, 140.

9. Davis, *History of Black Catholics*, 174.

10. Ibid., 173.

11. "Three Catholic Afro-American Congresses," *American Catholic Tribune* (1893).

12. Davis, *History of Black Catholics*, 193.

13. Agee, *Daniel Rudd*, 108.

Chapter Nine:
On to Chicago—pages 60–68

1. Edward R. Kantowicz, *The Archdiocese of Chicago: A Journey of Faith* (Booklink, 2006), 8.

2. Teresa Wiltz, "The Chicago Fire," *Chicago Tribune*, www chicagotribune.com/news/nationworld/politics/chi-chicagodays-fire -story-story.html.

3. "From Riots to Renaissance: Bronzeville: The Black Metropolis," WTTW, https://interactive.wttw.com/a/dusable-to-obama-explore -riots-to-renaissance-bronzeville-black-metropolis.

4. Charles J. Johnson and Marianne Mather, "Take a 'Walking Tour of the 1893 World's Columbian Exposition," www.chicagotribune .com/news/history/ct-the-white-city-20170503-htmlstory.html.

5. Quincy University Archives, Quincy, Illinois.

6. Ibid.

7. Archives of Josephites, Baltimore, Maryland.

8. Souvenir of silver jubilee of Archbishop Patrick Feehan (1891), 319–21.

9. *American Catholic Tribune* (November 1, 1890).

10. Ibid.

11. Ibid.

Chapter Ten:
Fellow Pioneer, Mother Katharine Drexel—pages 69–73

1. Cheryl C. D. Hughes, *Katharine Drexel: The Riches-to-Rags Life Story of an American Saint* (Grand Rapids, MI: Eerdmans, 2014), 11.

2. Archives of Blessed Sacrament Sisters, Bensalem, Pennsylvania.

3. Ibid.

4. Ibid.

Chapter Eleven:
St. Monica's Becomes a Reality—pages 74–82

1. Archives of the Josephites, Baltimore, Maryland.

2. *Quincy Daily Journal* (March 15, 1893).

3. Father Roy Bauer, "They Called Him Father Gus" (1997), part 27.

Chapter Twelve:
Final Days of Father Tolton and St. Monica's—pages 83–88

1. *Chicago Daily Tribune* (July 10, 1897).

2. Paul H. Geenen, *Milwaukee's Bronzeville: 1900–1950* (Charleston, SC: Arcadia, 2006).

Appendix 2:
Saint Augustus Tolton?—pages 95–98

1. "Father Tolton's cause is headed to the Vatican," *Catholic New World* (September 29, 2014).

2. "Father Tolton's cause takes next step forward," *Catholic New World* (December 26, 2016).

3. "The Cause for Sainthood of The Servant of God Reverend Augustus Tolton Continues to Advance with the Unanimous Approval of his Virtuous Life," Archdiocese of Chicago (February 13, 2019).

4. "Pope Francis elevates Augustus Tolton to 'venerable,'" *Chicago Catholic* (June 19, 2019).

Index